A SMILE, A TEAR, A MEMORY, A WISH

Helen Butterworth

*To Alan
With best wishes
Helen Butterworth.*

ARTHUR H. STOCKWELL LTD
Torrs Park   Ilfracombe   Devon
Established 1898
www.ahstockwell.co.uk

© *Helen Butterworth, 2012*
First published in Great Britain, 2012
All rights reserved.
*No part of this publication may be reproduced
or transmitted in any form or by any means,
electronic or mechanical, including photocopy,
recording, or any information storage and
retrieval system, without permission
in writing from the copyright holder.*

*British Library Cataloguing-in-Publication Data.
A catalogue record for this book is available
from the British Library.*

*Arthur H. Stockwell Ltd bears no responsibility
for the accuracy of information recorded in this book.*

*Every effort has been made to obtain the necessary permission with
reference to copyright material, both illustrative and quoted. We
apologise for any omissions in this respect and will be pleased to make
the appropriate acknowledgements in any future edition.*

ISBN 978-0-7223-4132-2
*Printed in Great Britain by
Arthur H. Stockwell Ltd
Torrs Park   Ilfracombe
Devon*

CONTENTS

Acknowledgements	4
To the Signature Tune of the BBC World Service	5
Five Years in Hanover	14
From Benghazi to the Land of the Pyramids	19
Demobilisation	25
VE Day	30
Searching for Roots	34
My Mother and Father	38
Childhood Days	43
The Waterproof Coat	46
Eleni	49
Schooldays	53
My Grandmother's Ordeal	60
The Unbearable Loss	65
A Lifelong Secret	70
The Lost Cousin George	75
The Forbidden Stones	85
The Stranger on the train	90
Rafina and the 2004 Olympics	96
A National Disaster	99
No Touch!	103
Why?	109
Junk Mail	112
Do Children's Stories Have a Moral Effect on Children?	116
Oblivion	119
Plato's Truth	122
False Alarm	125

TO THE SIGNATURE TUNE OF THE BBC WORLD SERVICE

I left Egypt on 15 November 1944, when the British Government decided to repatriate the families of servicemen who lived abroad. In my case it was Army Command who undertook the responsibility of bringing to the UK wives and families of soldiers who had married local girls while serving in Egypt.

I saw the lighthouse at Port Said becoming smaller and smaller until it disappeared as my ship sailed away to the unknown. The only time I had travelled abroad before was when I went to see relatives in Crete when I was only four years old. That holiday left me with three memories that have stayed with me ever since: the strong smell of a lemon tree in my auntie's garden; the howling of wolves on a night when we walked back to the village from the town in complete darkness; and falling out with my little cousin because I told her that my dinner plate had a prettier pattern on it than hers – I remember her crying, and I still feel guilty.

For the journey in 1944, an army lorry came to pick me up and take me from Ismailia (where I lived) to Port Said. There, I was going to join a number of other servicemen's wives who were also going to the UK. It was exactly eighteen months after my wedding. Our honeymoon was to have lasted two weeks, but we spent only the first five days together.

I climbed up and sat next to the driver of the army lorry. The sound of the engine starting brought to me the realisation that that was it! I was going away; I was leaving everybody and everything behind. My first feeling was one of anxiety – a feeling of fear rather than sadness for a few seconds. That was changed to deep remorse by the sight of the two figures, in black dresses, standing nearby to see me off, keeping back their tears with difficulty. I was leaving behind my mother, who had been widowed nine months earlier, and my recently divorced sister. The expression on their faces haunted me for a long time.

HMS *Queen of Bermuda*, a very large, luxury passenger ship, was waiting at Port Said for its unusual passengers. I had seen many similar ships before the war, passing along the docks of Port Said on their journey through the Suez Canal. They were often full of tourists, who would spread all over the town, buying souvenirs and seeing the sights. Merchant-navy ships would allow hundreds of sailors to spend the weekend on land, in their crispy white uniforms with the blue piping on the cuffs and collars.

HMS Queen of Bermuda.
(By courtesy The Dock Museum, Barrow-in-Furness – catalogue no 0830.)

The *Queen of Bermuda* was built in 1932 by Vickers-Armstrong and was originally used for service between New York and Bermuda. It could accommodate 700 passengers in first class, thirty-one in second class and had a crew of 410. In 1943 it was converted to a troopship and was used to bring troops home. One of its three original funnels was then removed, but it was restored again in 1949. It resumed its Bermuda service until 1961, when it was rebuilt with one funnel. In 1966 it was scrapped in Scotland.

For five weeks I shared a large cabin with three more young women: a pretty, blonde German Jewess; a beautiful Polish girl with black eyes and hair; and a very friendly Armenian girl. Their husbands were also on the ship, but mine, as far as I knew, was still serving in Europe.

My feelings were ever changing, affected not only by memories and anticipation but also by the circumstances under which I was travelling. There were times when the warm November sun on the top deck and the blue, calm waters of the Mediterranean Sea made me forget that an air raid could put an end to that unreal cruise at any time. The signature tune of the BBC World Service on the radio, the daily drill wearing life jackets to prepare the passengers for an emergency and the peeping through the blacked-out cabin windows were only a few of the things I remember that one would not experience during a cruise nowadays.

The awe-inspiring sight of the boundless, dark, mysterious sea, with nothing to be seen but the stars in the night sky, was something I shall never forget. Hundreds of young soldiers and women made up our disciplined but friendly community on board, and we were all looking forward to the end of the journey.

One of my saddest and most vivid memories of those days will always be the sound of sobbing that came from one of the berths in my cabin during one night. One of the young women, the wife of a teacher from Liverpool, the German

Jewess, had reached the loneliest point of her journey. I knew nothing of her background until the next day, when she confided in me. The memory of her father, who had died in a concentration camp not long before, was the cause of her grief. She also told me a story from her childhood, which perhaps reveals how she escaped from being placed into a concentration camp herself.

As a schoolchild she belonged to the generation which, in Germany, was taught that the Aryan race had an inborn superiority over other races. While the German children were being indoctrinated, often by visiting lecturers, the Jewish children were normally taken out of the classroom, but on one occasion she was present during one of those lectures. The speaker, after telling the children all about the superior qualities of the Aryan race, approached her, the Jewish child, and declared that she was a perfect example of the blonde, blue-eyed, fair-skinned Aryan child. Her classmates were very careful not to give away her secret.

The first stop of our ship was near Gibraltar, from where we could see the 'Rock' at a short distance. At that point some more ships with servicemen and wives joined our convoy, during the night, from Naples. My husband was in one of those ships. He was informed that I was on board one of the ships that had come from Egypt, and rather innocently he went to the captain of his ship and asked him if he could send a signal to the captain of my ship, asking him to inform me that he was coming home too. Of course the Captain knew better than to risk the possibility of the signal being intercepted by the enemy.

Our next stop was at Liverpool, where the convoy was split into two because Liverpool Docks could not cope with such a large number of ships. I heard later that the convoy consisted of forty vessels, with submarines and aeroplanes surrounding them for protection. One half of the convoy went on to Glasgow, while the passengers of the remaining ships were sent by train to their final destinations on a cold, sunny morning in December 1944.

Five weeks after I had left home in Egypt I found myself standing outside a railway station in Sheffield. It was a cold, wet and dark evening. Standing next to more luggage than I could possibly carry, I looked around for my husband's cousin, who had promised to come and meet me.

How could I have known that there were two railway stations in Sheffield – the LMS and the LNER? I stood on the pavement, wet, cold and miserable, waiting for my husband's cousin while the cousin was waiting just as anxiously at the other station.

Eventually I arrived at my destination. My husband's eighty-year-old 'Granny' was waiting for me in her pinafore. She was a very slim lady, with white, thick, wavy hair and she was very hard of hearing. Her four-storeys high, narrow terraced house was one of hundreds of houses in a long, steep street. There were two rooms on the ground floor, one large room on the first floor, and an attic and a cellar. The front room, next to the entrance, had been a small bakery before the war and Granny still kept it as a shop.

Granny at the entrance of her shop.

She had run the shop for many years while bringing up her four children after the death of her husband. She could still manage to bake some of her celebrated pies with rationed ingredients to serve her few remaining faithful customers. I am not sure whether she was entitled to any extra rations because of her little business. The few pies that she used to make were ordered in advance. She always made one for me too.

The conversation on that first evening was rather difficult (for me, shouting near her ear; and for her, probably struggling to understand my foreign accent). I was very touched by her gesture of moving to the attic and offering me her bedroom on the first floor. The cousin eventually arrived very worried, not knowing until then whether I had arrived at all.

The next morning I moved myself upstairs, into the attic, against Granny's protests.

My husband arrived in Sheffield from Glasgow two days later. We spent Christmas and a few more days with Granny. I had my first encounter with the English pub, where my husband took Granny and me one evening for an outing. Granny looked so smart in her best clothes and her necklace. It must have been her first social evening for a long time – at least for the five war years.

The smoky atmosphere of the pub, the strong smell of beer, the dimmed lights, the background music and the friendly, loud conversations between the customers, who were mainly men, were my first impressions when I stepped in. It was such a contrast to the cafés in Egypt, where families sat outside and watched people going and coming on a Saturday evening.

The rows of houses appearing to look exactly the same came as such a surprise to me. An outside toilet and a kitchen sink for all washing needs were not the only other surprises. The cousin, a really lovely person, 'adopted' me, and from the first minute she made it her duty to look after me. She took me to the shops, where I was fitted with clogs and a cape with hood attached. I was also given a giant black umbrella.

Granny in her smart clothes.

The first time I ventured to walk out in my new attire the steep pavement was frozen. I slipped forward on my heels, went flying and landed on my back. My pain was nothing compared to the embarrassment I felt while collecting my clogs from a few steps away. On another occasion I fell nearly all the way down the steep staircase when I was hurrying, wearing that gear, to open the door to the cousin.

Every Wednesday the cousin came to take me to chapel. Her friends were always waiting at the entrance for us to arrive, and then there was a ritual of embracing one another – a novelty I was not familiar with. They were all such lovely people. Why did I feel slightly irritated by this demonstration of their feelings for me? Even the vicar was welcoming – he placed a notice in the chapel *Chronicle* welcoming my husband and me.

At first people spoke to me more slowly and loudly than they would to anyone else, pronouncing every vowel very clearly, hoping that this would make it easier for me to understand what they thought I did not know. They also often asked me if I was thinking in Greek or in English. I could not answer that question even now. Does thinking have a language? I still use Greek when I multiply, but perhaps that is because it was the language in which I originally learned the times tables. I now think of the English alphabet when I search for a word in the dictionary, but for a long time I had to recite mentally the alphabet in French, because that was the language in which I first became familiar with the Roman version.

In Egypt women used to wear house gowns during the day. They were something between a dressing gown and a long dress. They were made of pretty materials, and one felt in them cool in the summer and warm in the winter as well as smart if facing an unexpected visitor. I had made myself one in a red woollen material with big black buttons down the front. Once when I walked out of the back door in my long gown I heard one of the two next-door neighbours saying to the other, "She is a lady." Later I connected that remark with what happened when Granny first heard that her 'sonny boy' was to marry a girl in Africa. All the neighbourhood was alerted, and who knows how they described me! When Granny received my wedding photograph she framed it and placed it in her shop window for all to see.

Granny developed a strong feeling for me as time passed. I reminded her of her young daughter, who had died ten years earlier from TB. She had been a secretary and played the piano. Granny never got over her death. I, in a way, had provided a replacement for her, but Granny developed a fear that she would lose me too. She became very jealous of the cousin, who in her opinion was trying to take me away from her.

My chapel outings and occasional visits to friends in the evening were a worry to her. She would not let me have a key to let myself in. The thought of a frail eighty-year-old sitting in her chair waiting for me to come back was spoiling my outings. I in my turn developed a fear of a very uncertain future waiting for me, as it was becoming more and more evident that the war was coming to an end.

FIVE YEARS IN HANOVER

When I received a form from my husband's army unit to fill in with my details and to sign, declaring that I had agreed to join him abroad, I could not complete it fast enough. I probably sent the form back the next day. There was no question in it relating to expectant wives and no indication of the leaving date. I soon had all my belongings packed back into the old linen trunk in which they had travelled all the way from Egypt to Sheffield about twenty-two months earlier.

I don't remember to which port the army transport took me to board the ship which was to take me to Germany to begin a new life with my husband, but one thing I do remember is the shock I felt when I realised that I was allocated the top bunk in a cabin with two bunk beds. I asked to see the ship's doctor in order to explain that in my condition climbing was slightly difficult.

The doctor just took a look at me and said, "You should not be here at all."

He explained to me that the limit for pregnant women to travel by sea was seven months; I was eight.

It was such a frightening moment. The thought of going back to Sheffield almost made me faint. The next few minutes, in which I tried to convince the doctor that I knew nothing about that limit, seemed like the longest in my life. The doctor eventually saw that it was not so much a matter of a stowaway passenger as an omission on the form; so he risked giving me permission to travel and offered me the lower bunk.

When I woke up next morning the ship had docked at Hamburg, and soon afterwards I was walking along the quay in my new loose camel coat. My husband was there waiting for me. Suddenly, photographers appeared out of the blue in front of us and asked us to embrace for the camera. It was so embarrassing – not so much because of the expected performance, but more because I was so much out of shape.

Sometime later my sister wrote to me that she and my mother were at the cinema on the following Saturday and they saw me arriving in Germany in the newsreel. I have often wondered if that film still exists. The reporters were not there for me personally, but because that ship was the first one to bring servicemen's families to Germany.

One month later, in November 1946, my son was the first BAOR baby. His original birth certificate said 'Born in Germany'. It was later reissued with the word Germany replaced by BAOR (British Army of the Rhine).

A flat had been prepared for us in Hanover in the north of West Germany. The city of Hanover was known before the war as 'The Garden of Europe'.

During the five years we lived in Hanover we saw the city rising from the ashes. Rebuilding had started almost immediately after the end of the war. Large areas were surrounded by high fences, and builders were working day and night. Within a year or so of the war shop windows were beautifully decorated for Christmas and other festivals.

For the army families there was the NAAFI – our army supermarket, on which we relied for food and through which we could order things to be sent from the UK. Our food was rationed and delivered by the NAAFI. I remember milk powder, egg powder, condensed milk and corned beef, all in set quantities. The Warrant Officers and Sergeants' Mess was the main source of entertainment for the families, with dancing, whist drives and parties for the children.

With hindsight I realise how sheltered life was for us. On the other hand the German people were living with the reality of the aftermath of destruction. Many German women were employed to work for the army families; they were paid partly by the army and partly by the servicemen.

We had Frieda, who became one of the family. Her own fifteen-year-old only child had been recruited and sent with thousands of other boys to the Russian Front, very near the end of the war, when Hitler was running short of men of fighting age. A young German soldier, who was lucky to survive, brought Frieda news from the front line about her son. They were together when her son was wounded in the leg. In those days the Russian Army did not give medical aid to wounded enemies. Frieda talked to her absent son every night before she went to sleep. She kept hoping that he was a prisoner of war somewhere in Russia and that one day he would come back. Later, she made herself believe that he was living somewhere happily with a Russian wife and a new family. She hung on to that hope until she died at the age of ninety-two. She was only thirty-eight when she lost her son. Her husband, Herman, whom we all called Papa, often came in the evenings and told stories to my (by then) two children, who learned to speak German as their second language long before the end of our five-year stay in Germany.

Frieda and Papa.

Soon after army families arrived in Germany, the army organised coach outings to East Berlin. During our outing we visited the 'bunker' in which Hitler died together with his family and members of his government. The concrete shelter was blown up after the end of the war. At that time very few people knew what had happened during the last days in the bunker, but there were a lot of rumours; visitors were free to let their imaginations roam to put the pieces of that puzzle in place.

On the same day we also visited the Chancellery, on the verandah of which Hitler stood and gave his famous speeches. I had seen films of Hitler in newsreels, waving his arms and shouting in a language so unfamiliar to me that I could not distinguish the end of one word from the beginning of the next. His small moustache will probably be always remembered as his most striking physical feature; the most striking example of his inhumanity was his anti-semitism. The walls of a very large room of the Chancellery were lined with glass mosaic tiles covered at the top with real gold. There had been a lot of looting by the invading armies and by souvenir seekers; the mosaic had been broken up and there were pieces left on the floor.

Hitler's chancellery.

On the way back to West Germany the coach stopped on the east side of the Brandenburg Gate, where East and West Germany met. There at the ground floor of a corner building was situated a jewellery shop where we bought a four-piece silver-plated dressing-table set. I thoughtlessly picked up the hairbrush and ran it through my hair. I had already made up my mind to purchase it, but the shopkeeper did not guess my good intentions. His loud shouting and the waving of his arms startled me, and for a second I imagined him with a little moustache – although he was a man of a much larger build than Hitler. I supposed he did not want to be left with a used hairbrush. We also bought at the same shop a set of mah-jongg, a Chinese game, which we often enjoyed playing with friends after dinner.

The day after our outing the Russians declared East Berlin out of bounds to the rest of the Allies. Germany was parted into zones after the war; East Berlin was in the zone allocated to Russia. Our coach was the last tourist coach allowed to visit East Berlin for a very long time. We heard that the next coach was stopped at the Brandenburg Gate and turned back. The construction of the Berlin Wall followed. This kept many East Berliners separated from relatives and friends for several years, until the wall was finally demolished and Germany became one unified country again.

Not long after we left Germany in 1952 a long article was published in *The Times* about Hanover. The city was referred to as 'the pre-war garden of Europe'. It was rebuilt very much as it was before the war.

During all the time we had spent in Hanover we only came across friendly and helpful people.

The gold covered mosaic.

FROM BENGHAZI TO THE LAND OF THE PYRAMIDS

In our small, black Austin car there was just enough room in the back for my mother sitting between my two children of eight and ten, with me in the front passenger seat and my husband driving. In this way we arrived in Alexandria on a hot Thursday afternoon in the summer of 1956. It had been a long journey from Benghazi – a seaside town in Libya – to Egypt, through the Sahara Desert. This was to be the beginning of a holiday my family and I had planned for a long time. I had left Egypt, as an army wife, twelve years earlier.

We intended to tour the city of Alexandria, named after Alexander the Great, visit its beaches and cool ourselves in the blue, clear water of the Mediterranean Sea; to taste the delicious fresh dates and the sweet watermelons; to visit the open-air cafés in the evenings; to drink the ice-cold lemonade and to eat the cashew nuts sold by the little Arab boys; to see a film at an open-air cinema under a starry sky; and to hear the Mohammedan muezzin call the faithful to prayer from the minaret of the mosque, which was done every evening before sunset.

Two or three days were to be spent in Alexandria before we carried on our journey along the north coast of Egypt to the Suez Canal, where we planned to spend a day in Port Said. Here is the narrowest point of the Suez Canal, which parts the continents of Africa and Asia. We thought we might even catch the ferry and sail across to the little town of Port-Fouâd, with its beautiful beach and picturesque cottages, which were built by the Suez

Canal Company for its employees.

The Suez Canal is a narrow strip of water which stretches from Port Said, a town on the north coast of Egypt on the Mediterranean Sea, to Suez on the Red Sea coast. The Suez Canal is 103 miles long, and at its narrowest point it is 196 feet wide. The Pharaohs tried unsuccessfully to build a canal here; and the Romans tried too, but the project was abandoned after the fall of the Roman Empire. The Egyptians excavated a canal in the seventeenth century, but it had to be filled in again to stop illegal traffic using it.

After another 300 years Napoleon ordered a survey of the Isthmus of Suez. It was found that the level of the Red Sea was much higher than that of the Mediterranean Sea, but this finding was proved to be wrong later. In 1859 the Suez Canal Company began work under its French engineer Ferdinand de Lesseps. The building of the Suez Canal took ten years. It opened on 17 November 1869. Ships could pass through the canal in eleven and a half hours.

Nearly 100 years later we were planning to visit Port Said and then to carry on to the small town of Ismailia, where my married life had begun in 1943.

Our next excursion was going to be an exciting visit to the Pyramids, just outside Cairo, the capital city of Egypt. I had in the past described these giant stone monuments, together with the Sphinx, to my children. They expected to see bigger stones than they had ever seen before; they were going to sit on camels and be taken for a ride by Arab guides wearing long white robes, with turbans on their heads and sandals on their feet.

We talked about all these things as we set off from Benghazi on the three-day journey to Alexandria. They were three long days of excitement and expectation for the children; three long days of hard driving through the steaming, hot sand of the Sahara Desert for my husband. For my mother it meant coming back to the land she had grown to consider to be her second home – to the country which forty-five years earlier opened its arms to receive many Greek refugees from Asia Minor.

My feelings were mixed. I was apprehensive about the changes I might find. My memories of carefree, cosmopolitan, pre-war Egypt were every now and then torn by the sight of rusting tanks. They had been abandoned in the desert after meeting with disaster on their way to El Alamein during the Second World War.

We had left Benghazi on a Tuesday morning and by the evening of the same day we reached Tobruk. There were very few villages in this part of Libya, which is within the Sahara Desert. We spent the night at a hotel. There, we ate some most delicious doughnuts – a speciality for which the couple running the hotel had acquired some fame. We slept in a very large room, on five ex-army beds.

It took us all next day to arrive at Mersa Matruh, a pleasant seaside town on the Egyptian border.

We drove straight to the customs office to have our passports stamped and our luggage inspected. We were hoping to go as speedily as possible through these formalities. We intended to spend a relaxing afternoon on the beach before booking into a hotel for the night.

The customs office was closed because Wednesday was closing day. The possibility of tourists arriving there on a Wednesday was apparently no reason to keep it open. A warden, who was sitting outside the building, left his chair reluctantly and, at an unperturbed pace, walked away to bring the customs official from his home. Our intrusion cost us one extra pound besides the two-hour delay.

Mersa Matruh was crowded with rich Egyptians on holiday, moving about in big American cars and speaking to one another in French. French was the recognised international language of this country, which was inhabited by people of all nationalities. It was a visiting place for tourists, sailors and commercial seamen from all over the world.

Another memory I shall always treasure is of our stop at El

Alamein. It was like visiting a village of the dead. Thousands of soldiers fell during the Battle of El Alamein in the Second World War, when the Allied forces under Field Marshal Montgomery confronted the German Afrika Corps. On entering the British cemetery, one is faced with neat rows of gravestones extending in all directions almost as far as the eye can see. There is an imposing, very tall cross standing on the top of an oblong stone building at the other end of the cemetery opposite the entrance. Further along the same road are the German and the Italian war cemeteries. There are also the South African war cemetery and other memorials.

The British cemetery at El Alamein.

During the entire journey the weather was hot and very uncomfortable. Sitting in the car was like being in an oven, and it was of no use opening the windows and letting in the hot desert air.

We wasted no time at all once we finally arrived at Alexandria early on Thursday afternoon. We had a quick wash and hurried out towards the seafront for some fresh air. By that time it was around five o'clock and the sun was a little more bearable. We soon noticed that crowds of people were gathering and standing along both sides of the main road.

We joined the crowd, not having the slightest idea that what we were going to witness was one of the most important events since the Battle of El Alamein. The procession arrived headed by police cars and still more police cars, followed by a military Jeep. In this car, Gamal Abdel Nasser, the President of Egypt, was standing, waving his arms to the cheering crowds. I noticed, as the car was passing in front of us, that he wore a bulletproof jacket that made him look larger than he really was.

We realised that something very special was happening, although we knew that the Egyptians had no particular annual celebrations on that date. We returned to the hotel in a great hurry. There the radio was blazing away: a speech by President Nasser was being broadcast. He had just announced that he had on that day taken over the administration of the Suez Canal, which had been under British administration for the past eighty years. He had suddenly seized the Suez Canal for Egypt. For the Egyptian people it was a day of national pride. They were too happy to think about any possible adverse implications.

We spent a sleepless night listening to continual announcements competing with the loud Eastern music in the background. At the same time a profusion of fireworks was being let off from the flat rooftops of surrounding houses to add to the pandemonium.

Early next morning a representative of the secret police came to the hotel asking for us. They already knew a lot about us. He was reassured that we were there on a short holiday and he left. My husband went immediately to the British Embassy, where, together with several other visitors to the country, he was advised to return to Benghazi as soon as possible.

Back into the car went our luggage, most of which we had not had time even to open since it was inspected by the customs official at the border.

Very early on Saturday morning we were on our way out of Alexandria, travelling much faster than we had driven on our way in. We did not wish to spend another night on that side of the Egyptian frontier. We were more than thankful when this time we found the customs office open.

On our way back we were stopped by sentries, who were placed along the route at frequent intervals. Each time we had to show our passports, and we were afraid that we might be arrested. We knew that the political situation was deteriorating by the minute, and as the batteries of our radio had run out, we were imagining the worst.

We would have arrived at the frontier uneventfully if we had not taken the wrong turning in the desert. We suddenly realised that the road on which we were travelling had come to an end. With a feeling of dismay at wasting precious time, we turned the car round and started back again. Suddenly we noticed a big, heavy lorry coming towards us. On this lorry were standing several Arab men who appeared to be labourers. When they were at a distance of only a few yards, one of them lifted a machine gun and pointed it towards our car. Before we had time to panic, the incident was over.

Things were happening so fast that only later did it occur to us that they might have suspected us of being spies. When the lorry was near enough for the men to see that the occupants of our car were the driver, two women and two children, they stopped and greeted us with the warm humour, typical of the people of the Nile, that I had known for many years. We all laughed and each vehicle went on its way. The lorry took the labourers to the dead end of the road to continue their work under the scorching sun. They explained to us that they were building a new road, which was to end at a new oasis, somewhere in the Sahara Desert.

We were now driving faster than ever. We arrived at Tobruk very tired but very relieved that night. Early next morning we were on our way back home to Benghazi. The first thing we wanted to do when we entered our house, thirsty and exhausted, was to taste some of the fresh figs which we had placed in the boot of the car before we left Alexandria. This fruit normally has a delightful smell and flavour, but the figs had perished in the heat of the Sahara Desert. The whole box had to be thrown away. We had only tasted one each when the large box was placed in a hurry in the boot of the car.

DEMOBILISATION

We had only been for eighteen months at Krefeld in Germany when my husband all of a sudden had a diabetic blackout. This resulted in his having to retire from army service, and our overseas tour was ended abruptly. After a month at the hospital my husband was demobilised and we came back to England with our three children aged thirteen, eleven and eighteen months. This was in February 1960.

We spent three months at the Royal Pier Hotel in Southsea. It was our second stay at this beautiful hotel, which was then taken over by the army and was used for warrant officers between tours abroad or making the transition to civilian life. The hotel was facing the sea, and through our windows we could see every evening the funfair all lit up, with the big wheel in full swing. That February was such an unusually warm month that the fair had opened much earlier than usual.

I heard people referring to the 'Royal Suite' and I was told that King Edward VIII broadcast his abdication speech to the nation from his rooms in the hotel before he left to join Mrs Wallis Simpson. She was the woman he loved and for whom he gave up the throne because his family and his Church could not accept her as their queen. She was a Catholic and a divorcee.

Those three months of paid leave were, on hindsight, one of the most carefree periods we had had for many years. I spent many hours reading in the Sunken Gardens, opposite the hotel, while my little son was having his afternoon nap in his pram. My two older children were accepted at the two grammar schools of Portsmouth. They had passed the Marray test in army schools abroad – it was the equivalent of the then eleven-plus.

As time passed we knew that we would soon have to look for a house to buy. We loved Southsea and our wish was to settle down there after retirement. One day we saw an advertisement for a house that sounded ideal for us. The address wasn't given, but we dialled the number and were directed to a house only a short way from the hotel, in a terrace of beautiful buildings with only the green common between it and the seafront.

"Surely we cannot afford this," I said to my husband just as an elderly lady answered the bell and asked us in.

We soon realised that the house we had just arrived at was not the one for sale. It belonged to the lady, as did the estate agency, which was run by her son. She was very friendly to us and loving to our little boy. She offered to take him in his pram for walks and hinted that she would be our friend for life. She was a little overpowering, with her interest in our situation and with her desire to help an army family with young children in rather urgent need of accommodation. It was a little difficult for us, facing for the first time the complications of buying a house in this country. The army had provided us with comfortable accommodation for about fifteen years, but that had been abroad.

Our host eventually took us to see the house for sale, after cups of tea and biscuits. We felt by then that she genuinely wanted to help us.

The house was 150 years old, on three levels, with large rooms, high ceilings and open fireplaces. It was within five minutes' walk of the seafront. It was one of many tall, narrow terraced houses in a long street. We moved in and soon grew very fond of it. I particularly loved the two attic rooms with windows in the sloping roof.

We were able to use some of the rooms for bed-and-breakfast accommodation in the summer. The work was very tiring, but it was also very interesting. The guests were mainly pensioners who had travelled to the South Coast from Yorkshire or from Wales.

We lived happily for eighteen months in that house until one morning we were woken up by a lot of noise. A crowd of people had gathered in the street outside, and we were told that the whole front of a house a few doors away had collapsed.

One of the neighbours said to me, "It has happened to other houses in this road. They were built on wet ground and there is salt in the sand used to build them."

That information caused us considerable anxiety, to which was added the fear of the heavy original ceilings collapsing. This did not take long to happen. One morning when he was assembling a bed in one of the two attic rooms, my husband accidentally dropped a heavy tool on the floor. The ceiling of the bedroom underneath fell in with a mighty noise. The two single beds of that bedroom were covered with pieces of plaster, large and small, and everything was under thick dust. Only one hour earlier two old ladies had vacated the room at the end of their week's holiday in Southsea.

I spent many hours, after that, in the night worrying that the front wall of the house might decide to fall and also worrying about my children's safety sleeping under those heavy old ceilings. Once again I started looking in estate agents' windows, and, as my husband was then working at an army depot outside Portsmouth, the thought of living in the country became more and more appealing to me. I naively thought that any place outside a big town could be considered to be 'country'.

When I came across an advertisement for a bungalow for sale outside Portsmouth, I thought it sounded ideal for us. My husband would have a much shorter distance to drive to work;

my mother, who was then living with us, would enjoy being busy in the garden; and my little son would benefit in a few months' time from the infant school, which was just next door. There was an orchard of apple and pear trees in the garden and, when we moved in, we even bought some chickens to give an added interest to him and his grandmother, with whom he was going to be left during the day when the rest of us were at work or at school.

That move proved to be a disaster. It took place during the worst winter that this country had had for many years: 1962/3. There was a lot of snow, and it remained on the ground for a long time, causing icy roads until the end of March. The woods nearby became too muddy to visit with the pram, our garden was waterlogged and the chickens were up to the neck in mud. There was no joy in going outside to pick up the eggs.

I was then working at Southsea, producing a weekly magazine for the local branch of John Lewis. The return journey to and from work by bus, together with the lunch break, was taking nearly three hours out of my day. Life became very lonely for my mother – especially when my little son started school next door and she was on her own all day. My two teenage children also felt isolated. They had left all their friends behind, and Cowplain had nothing to offer to teenagers who were too young to venture to the city and back in the evenings. Besides, there was the added expense of bus fares for them going to school and me going to work. We were not really 'living' in the country, but more like struggling to survive in it.

When it was announced that the WD depot was moving to new premises in Gosport, we knew it was an opportunity to move again for the sake of us all. The chickens were given to a neighbour, the apples and pears had not yet had enough sunshine to ripen, and the teacher at the infant school next door sent a message to say that she was sorry to lose her new pupil after only one term at the school.

Sunny Southsea was ours again to enjoy.

I remained in Southsea for forty-five years. Then, as I was now left on my own, far away from all my family, I decided to move to Cambridge in order to be nearer to at least some of them. And so this time I moved from sunny Southsea to the city of beautiful architecture and academic excellence.

VE DAY

On Monday 7 May 1945 Germany surrendered to the Allied forces. At one minute after midnight the papers were finally signed by representatives of both sides. Later in the morning Sir Winston Churchill appeared outside his offices in Whitehall, after his speech had been broadcast by radio to the nation. He had his famous cigar in his mouth while with his right hand he was giving the victory sign to an estimated 50,000 cheering people.

According to the *Daily Mirror* of 8 May, London morning newspapers gave the day off to their staff, so there were no newspapers published next day in London, and the 8th and 9th of May were declared public holidays. On 8 May the first official weather forecast was issued since the outbreak of the war: 'Warm or very warm, with continuous thunderstorms or thundery rain'.

The headline of the *Daily Mirror* of 8 May was 'VE Day! Public Holiday Today and Tomorrow'. The letters VE stand for Victory in Europe. The headline of the same paper on the 9th was 'Britain's Day of Rejoicing'. It was placed above a photograph of the crowds in Whitehall with Sir Winston Churchill standing among them.

On VE day I was in Sheffield, where I had lived for the previous six months. It was a Tuesday. I went to the office of the electric company where I worked, and I was told that I could go back home. What made me walk towards the city centre? I vividly remember walking through the streets of Sheffield among a crowd of people, which was getting thicker as new people were joining it, singing, laughing, cheering. I felt so lost among those happy people. I had never felt so lonely before. It is true that one can feel alone in a crowded place.

Thousands of people who had lost loved ones in the war must have had the same feeling as I had on that day. I was lucky enough not to have received the dreaded telegram that relatives used to receive after the death of a serviceman. Sir Winston Churchill wrote in his memoirs of VE day 'Apprehension for the future and many perplexities filled my mind as I moved among the cheering crowds.' These words could describe exactly my state of mind during a day when everyone's wish had come true after five long years of war. My husband was in Europe, and my own family was a whole world away.

Granny, with whom I had been living since I left my family in Egypt, was over eighty. One of her sons had died from gas poisoning after the First World War. I wanted very much to go back to her, but I had no idea where I was or which way to turn. I discovered that walking against the tide of the crowd was impossible. I have a faint recollection of jumping on a bus when the crowd started thinning out.

Sheffield, being an important industrial city, had been one of the main targets of enemy planes, but by the end of 1944 (when I arrived there) the raids had stopped. One sad memory, which has stayed with me, is the feeling that I had every morning walking towards the electric-company offices after leaving the bus at the corner of the square. In front of me was a large space of ground covered in rubble; it was just one of many similar bomb sites in the city. There were often bunches of flowers placed on the ground at these sites. I found out later that a big public house used to be on the corner of the square where the rubble was. When the bomb hit the building there were 200 people in that pub. They took their last drink on that night.

With the end of the war came the end of an uncertainty that had almost become a way of life. Duty and survival were the main priorities during the five years of the war. One had to live according to decisions that one could not dispute. The giant puzzle that the war had broken up had to be put together again by the combined effort and sacrifice of millions of people. Their own individual puzzles had become incomplete when compulsory service, evacuation of children and general splitting-up of families became the norm of wartime.

Servicemen and women who had been mobilised at the beginning of the war started receiving their demobilisation papers. Those who already had academic or practical qualifications before the war were looking forward to carrying on from where they had left off. Perhaps a short refresher course would help some to revitalise the family business. Others would try to earn money using skills they had acquired in wartime service – such as car repairing, road and bridge building, plumbing, electrical engineering, bookkeeping, nursing and other occupations.

On the other hand, lack of experience and the uncertainty of the situation made many men decide to stay in the forces, where their wartime learning was still useful. For my husband and me a choice had to be taken quickly between staying on in the army or coming out and facing civilian life. We longed for a normal family life with a home of our own, but we could see no possibility of that materialising in the immediate future. I had already spent two years in Sheffield, but I had not put down deep enough roots to keep me there. I had no stable background to rely on while preparing for an independent start.

As an alternative, the army offered security for the families of service personnel – accommodation and good pay. It also offered the opportunity of seeing the world, which was an opportunity few young people otherwise had. Even travelling by train in pre-war Egypt was quite a rare treat for ordinary people. I remember that the return fare from Egypt to Crete was £5 in the late thirties. A qualified accountant was then earning £6 per month and an office clerk £2. To put this into perspective, I should perhaps add that the price of the *Daily Mirror* was just one penny on VE day, and there were 240 pennies in the pound in those days.

The decision to stay on in the army was made by us when we realised that our first child was due in November 1946. My husband was lucky enough to be given a posting to West Germany, where families were allowed to join their husbands. The war with Japan had not ended yet, and many servicemen were posted to the Far East, leaving their wives and families behind once more.

A comfortable flat was prepared for us in Kleefeld, a suburb of Hanover and that was our home for the next five years.

SEARCHING FOR ROOTS

My husband joined the army as an eighteen-year-old in 1938 mainly to escape an unhappy childhood. So far life had not opened its arms to the young man. He had found himself in a children's home at the age of four. His mother was suddenly out of his life, and a void was left in him which was to affect the rest of his life.

The loss of his mother, and his rejection by other relatives, was beyond his understanding at that age. He must have wondered what had happened, and visitors who came to see other children in the home must have added to his bewilderment. At the same time, other children must have remarked on his lack of visitors.

My husband had a very faint memory of his mother. He remembered that at some time, very early in his life, he went to a house where he slept between two people who loved him, gave him toys and took him out of the children's home a few times.

Three or four years followed when nobody appeared. Then, when he was ten, all of a sudden he discovered what he had been wondering about for years. A cloth bag with his name on it had hung on the back of the door for as long as he could remember. One day he took the bag down and inside he found a piece of paper with an address on it. For a few days he thought over his next step, and at last he summoned up a great courage and walked out of the home. He asked passers-by the way to the address, which he had by then learned by heart, and he eventually found himself outside the house where he had shared a bed with a loving couple when he was very young. They lived there with an older lady – it was the lady he was eventually to know as 'Granny'. After this, the young boy was allowed to visit the house regularly, but he was abandoned again when the man, who was Granny's son, died as a result of gas poisoning which he had sustained during the First World War. The visits stopped and loneliness lasted until the young boy was thirteen years old. Then he ran away again, with nowhere to go this time.

It was getting dark when he found himself in front of a farm. He knocked at the door and asked the man who opened it if he needed some help on the farm. The farmer took him in, and his wife put in front of him a very good and welcome meal.

They gave him a comfortable bed to sleep in, but in the morning, when the boy thought he would at last start work and become independent, there was a knock on the door during breakfast. The farmer had informed the police about the boy, and two policemen had come to take him back to the home. The farmer had done what he believed to be his duty, but to the desperate boy it was yet another rejection.

The boy ran away every now and again until he was eighteen. Now he was able to make a choice for himself. He joined the regular army.

When I met him in 1942 he was the youngest sergeant in the Royal Engineers. He was serving in the office of the headquarters where I was employed as a typist. A year later we were married in the Garrison Church, in Moascar, which was the army camp in Ismailia, where the headquarters of the Royal Engineers was. Five days later on 20 May 1943 my husband was called back to his unit. Our honeymoon of two weeks was cut down to five days.

In complete secrecy the Royal Engineers were preparing to leave North Africa for the landings on the south coast of Italy.

Getting married in the Garrison Church, in Moascar.

They were to repair roads and bridges on their way northwards in preparation for the 1944 invasion of the north coast of Europe. I carried on working at the old headquarters, where a few remaining servicemen were doing the final packing-up in order to vacate the buildings.

About three weeks passed and I had not heard at all from my husband. On the third Saturday night I dreamed that there was a knock at the door. I opened the door and saw a transparent figure standing in front of me. At the same time I heard my husband's voice say, "I am leaving at one."

Next morning I decided to go to the camp, hoping to find out what had happened. I met the Sergeant, who had been the best man at our wedding. I did not mention my dream to him, but he realised that I was anxious because of the lack of news. He already knew that the unit had gone to Cairo. He said he would go to Cairo in the afternoon to try to find out what was happening, and he promised to let me know the next day.

On Monday morning when we met at the camp he told me that when he arrived at a big building in Cairo all the doors were open and there were notices on each door saying 'Top Secret – Out of Bounds'. There was not a soul there except for a guard at the entrance.

When the guard was asked where everyone was he answered, "They left at one."

The unit had left on the night of my strange dream.

Outside the Royal Engineers Headquarters at Moascar.

My parents in 1914.

MY MOTHER AND FATHER

My mother was born in 1890 in Alatsata, a town near Smyrna in Asia Minor. This is the part of Turkey facing mainland Greece with the Aegean Sea between them. She was one of thirteen children and belonged to a family of farmers. Her father and older brothers worked at their farm at Tsesme, a short distance from their home. The names of many places in Turkey have since been replaced by Turkish names.

Asia Minor was controlled by Greece in ancient times. The Temple of Artemis was one of the Seven Wonders of the Ancient World, and other famous ancient sites still attract visitors from all over the world. The origins of Smyrna, the second town in Asia Minor, have been placed mythologically in the fourteenth century BC; historically they are placed towards the end of 1,000 BC. It is one of the towns reputed to be the birthplace of Homer – where his poems were first recited. My mother's ancestors lived there for a very long time and considered their country as part of Greece.

As well as tourism, a thriving commerce grew up around the ports of Asia Minor. Its Aegean coast was visited by ships transporting important goods between the East and the West.

It was customary in Asia Minor for only the first daughter to go to school for basic education in reading and writing, but an exception was made for my mother, who was the second daughter. Sadly, this was short-lived. She remembered her mother saying,

"My little girl is back from school; the house smells so good!" Little did she know that her little girl had spent the day at the farm with her father and brothers.

The main occupation of the inhabitants of that part of the country was farming. The family owned fields and farmhouses and produced mainly raisins and tobacco. The natural beauty of the surroundings and the well-being that the family enjoyed from the income their business provided was often reflected in their nostalgic memories years later.

Once I asked my mother what it was like at her home, and she answered, "We had a big house, opposite the church, with a balcony and there was a mosaic in front of the entrance."

On another occasion I was told that the area was covered by green low hills with windmills on their tops and high mountains in the background.

Five members of my grandmother's family were drowned on their way back from France, and this tragedy put an end to my mother's longing to go back to Asia Minor.

My mother met my father in Egypt, and they were married in Alexandria in 1914. I was born in that city in 1921. My sister was seven years older than me, and there were two more children between us two; they died during the First World War from malnutrition. I have an old icon of St George, on the back of which my father has written '10th of October, 1917, Thursday, Dionisios was born at 7 pm'.

During the difficult years of the First World War my father managed to get employment with a firm which sold Greek newspapers and magazines in Alexandria. The firm owned a piece of land on which there was a small wooden house, and we lived there rent-free in exchange for my parents' keeping an eye on the land.

It was probably by a stroke of good luck that my father was later offered the running of an agency selling Greek newspapers and magazines at Port Said in Egypt. I was two and half years old then.

My father, who was born in a remote village high on a mountain in the Peloponnese in 1872, has always been a wonder to me. How did he manage to run his business successfully for about twenty years? He had only had a basic primary-school education.

I must have been around eight when he started dictating to me his business letters, which he used to sign and seal with red wax into which he would press a ring that had his initials on the top. He always wore this ring on his little finger. I used to help him to unpack the big, heavy parcel that arrived from Piraeus every Wednesday. It contained papers, magazines and any books my father might have ordered.

Each paper had to be individually assembled, folded and placed on a counter. At the end of the month, all papers and magazines that were left unsold had to be packed and sent back to Piraeus, the port of Athens, where the headquarters of the business was situated.

Wednesday was my favourite day of the week. I would wait anxiously to catch up with the serial stories in the magazines and also to read the headlines of the papers. Politics has always been ingrained in the Greeks, especially in the ones who live abroad. I remember angry comments exchanged between two men sitting outside an open-air café.

My father was a staunch royalist to the point of giving my younger brother the name of the then King of Greece after having given me the name of the mother of another famous Greek king, Emperor Constantine, the founder of Constantinople. Constantine and Helen are celebrated as saints on 21 May. On that day in 1943, six days after my wedding, my mother received visitors to celebrate my and my brother's name day. My husband was called back by his unit the day before; my brother had gone to work for the British in East Africa.

Until my brother reached school age, my father was helped by my young uncle, who, with his mother, had come to Port Said to live with us. When he was eighteen years old he married a young woman who was also a refugee from Asia Minor and

My father's helper.

they went their own way. My mother was then able to help my father by sitting in the shop while he went on his bicycle to deliver orders of papers and magazines. My sister left school at fourteen; she attended the last class before further classes were approved by the Ministry of Education in Greece. She learned dressmaking, which was then a good occupation. Most women either made their own clothes or had them made by a dressmaker.

Our shop occupied the front room in a ground-floor flat of a two-storey building. The second room had a table and chairs and was used as our dining room. The third room was the kitchen. There my mother used to prepare delicious meals on a paraffin stove while she was keeping an eye on the shop. There were no fridges at that time; we had what was called an icebox, which was lined with a metal sheet. I remember a man delivering a big column of ice. He carried it on his shoulder, walking very fast through the flat, and placed it in the icebox after wrapping it in pieces of hessian cloth. Perishable food was kept in the icebox, and other food was kept in a cabinet which had wire mesh on its door.

I remember trying to teach my mother to read, but she did not get any further than being able to write her name. Nevertheless she developed to perfection a method of her own, which we might call today 'look and read'. If the customer asked for a particular paper or magazine she could identify it by the shape of its name on the front page.

Except for a young Egyptian boy who ran errands for us and a woman who came to wash the clothes, all the housework was done by my mother. My sister and I helped on Saturday mornings, and we were expected to look after our bedroom, which we shared. On Saturday afternoons we three went to the cinema. That was usually a family outing. Babies in prams, small children running about during the intervals, those who could read explaining what was going on on the screen, people shelling peanuts or unwrapping sweets – these were all part of the afternoon's entertainment.

I doubt whether there were many cowboy films that we missed, and we probably saw nearly all the silent films of Charlie Chaplin and Laurel and Hardy, whom we knew as 'the fat one and the thin one'. There were subtitles on the two sides of the screen in Greek and French. It was pandemonium, but nobody minded. On Sunday afternoons, after enjoying a special Sunday meal, the three of us would walk through the city to the statue of de Lesseps, wearing our Sunday clothes, and we would walk the length of the road which runs alongside the Suez Canal.

Those were our winter weekends. In the summer the long beach of Port Said used to claim most of the population of the city – especially during the long school holidays, which lasted from the middle of June to the first Monday in October.

My mother at the beach hut, Port Said.

CHILDHOOD DAYS

My mother was a well-organised person, doing her jobs on set days. Every time I wash my hair or cut my nails on the wrong day – 'wrong' as far as she was concerned – I think of her and her wise saying, which rhymes in Greek: "Don't cut your nails on Wednesday or on Friday, and don't wash your hair on a Sunday if you want to do well in life." This was one of many sayings that my mother used to come out with.

I was surprised when I first came to England to find that many of her sayings were used here too, like the one about the bird in the hand, albeit with a slight variation. The Greek version is 'Better one in the hand than ten and waiting for them.' Many superstitions are also shared by the two countries – for example, not to walk under a ladder, to cross one's fingers, or to throw salt over one's shoulder.

Religious belief, respect or even fear also played a big part in people's lives. I was brought up never to sit with icons behind me. As a child I thought that I would be punished if I did. I know now that it was a mark of respect.

There was always in the main bedroom a shelf on the wall with some icons of saints on it. In the middle was placed a plate with a glass three-quarters full of water, and on the top was a small amount of oil. On the oil was floating a tiny candle attached to a small base with pieces of cork glued underneath. It was called '*candili*'. The candle was lit every evening and it would last until morning. I remember standing in front of this shelf before going to bed and saying the Lord's Prayer. I would end by making the sign of the Cross, moving my hand from my forehead to my chest and from my right shoulder to my left and asking God to keep my family well, naming them one by one and adding any other people who were dear to me. After jumping into bed I would feel my mother tucking me in as I pretended that I was asleep. We had to be in bed by eight o'clock, before my father came back from the shop.

The votive candle (candili) and icon of St George.

There was no set time for closing shops. It all depended on whether a passenger ship was expected to arrive at the port – and they could come at any time. We often went to the city in the evening to see the big luxury ships and the tourists, as well as the sailors, visiting the big shops and buying souvenirs. There were special landing places at the quay for them, with temporary bridges stretched between the ship and the land. The main streets were lit up, the open-air cafés were open, and there was a festive atmosphere enjoyed both by the tourists and by the local people.

When I was old enough to be left in the shop while my father delivered the orders, I could not wait for him to come back. Then, with my sun hat on and a halfpenny to buy peanuts, I would make my way to the beach about half a mile away. A short distance from my destination there was a road of beautiful big houses. They belonged to executives of the Suez Canal Company. One of these houses had gained the reputation of being haunted.

I was determined to solve the mystery, but I remember quickening my pace as I passed in front of it looking closely at its windows in the hope of catching a glimpse of the ghost. I am sure it was not my imagination working overtime when, one day, I spotted, next to a curtain pulled to one side, the face of an old man with white hair and a long, thick white beard. He was looking at me with a friendly smile – but that did not stop me from running as fast as I could.

Very few people owned cars in the thirties in Egypt – especially in smaller towns like Port Said. I only knew of three men who had their own cars and they were all doctors. Trams and horse-drawn coaches took people everywhere. Children met with friends in the morning and walked to school together. The older children looked after the younger ones.

Not many people could afford to go abroad on holiday in those days, but the Suez Canal Company employees could go every so many years to visit their relatives in Greece, with all expenses paid by the company.

There was a distinct middle class of professional and business people – a class of people with ordinary jobs who earned a reasonably good living; and there were poor people who had no income and relied on organisations run by the better-off community. At my school there were breakfasts for the children of the poorer families every morning. Regular voluntary donations are still given to help the poor in Greece. At funerals only relatives give flowers. Friends give money to philanthropic organisations instead. Churches also help the poor. On the opposite side of the road from my father's shop there was a Catholic church. Every Friday afternoon people went in, and came out with parcels in their hands.

There was no free health service and no benefits for any people, but there were collections of clothes for the poor and one would see people begging outside the churches and the big shops. The influx of refugees from Asia Minor and other countries after the First World War caused difficulties in Egypt for a long time.

THE WATERPROOF COAT

As a child all I knew about my father's past was that he was born at a village called Georgitsi, near Sparta, on the Peloponnese, which is the southern peninsula of mainland Greece.

My father was a real Spartan, a man of few words and even fewer possessions. The Spartan fighting spirit was there if only in his love for hunting and fishing. His affection for his hunting dog came second only to his love for his family and for his best friend, Basil.

Basil was a tall, quiet, elderly man with a thick, white moustache, rolled up neatly at the ends. Basil worked at the small dockyard used by the ferry boats which took the Suez Canal workers from Port Said to Port Fouâd at the southern end of the canal. Basil came every evening and sat with my father outside our shop until eight o'clock, when it was closing time.

My father used to go fishing on the side of a jetty after the ferries had stopped their journeys in the evenings. Once, just as he was reaching his usual fishing spot, on a moonless night in November, he took a step sideways and found himself in the water. Basil was not on duty that night – a fact that my father did not know. He would not let go of his fishing implements and he could not swim. He held his fishing stool in one hand and his fishing gear in the other, and he sank to the bottom of the water. He somehow surfaced before he ran out of breath and started calling, "Vassili, Vassili! Help!"

There was no answer from his friend Basil.

He submerged again and almost gave up hope that he would be rescued. It was dark and cold, the whole port was deserted and he could not swim.

I remember my mother saying to a friend that he started praying and suddenly found himself floating on the surface of the water with his waterproof coat spread like a sheet under him supporting his body. He was still holding on to his fishing gear. He kept on calling for help until a patrolling guard heard him and came to his rescue. This happened on 29 November – the eve of St Andrew's Day. People considered it a miracle. However, what would have happened without the waterproof coat? The fishing stool is still one of my treasured possessions.

Hunting – my father's other hobby – was permitted by law only at the cemetery outside the town of Port Said. I loved going there with my father. Our dog, Mavros – or Blacky – would retrieve the shot birds, while I would spend much of the time walking around the cemetery, reading the inscriptions on the tombstones and trying to imagine what the deceased people might have been like. Some of the tombstones had photographs on them, and sad personal comments.

There were some elaborate tiny buildings in the shape of one-room chapels. These were vaults for the remains of members of rich families. I remember looking through the keyholes, expecting to see bodies. The combined feelings of awe and curiosity, accompanied by the incessant buzzing of bees in a heaven of wild flowers, are inseparable from my memories of those rather strange day-outings with my father and his dog.

After Mavros died he was replaced by Leon, a brown-and-white retriever. He lived in the room at the back of our shop and joined the family every Sunday in our flat. He was then placed, with his basket, food and water, on the balcony in a shaded spot. He was a pet, but not in the way that pets are considered today. He was, however, my father's most faithful friend. Every evening, before closing the shop, my father would pour milk into Leon's bowl, say goodnight to him and 'shake hands' with him, Leon offering his paw after he entered his basket.

When my father died, Leon joined the funeral procession. Without being noticed by anyone, he joined the mourners, and he walked behind the carriage and horses until somebody saw him and took him back home. By that time, 16 July 1942, we had moved to Ismailia, and the Orthodox Greek church was only ten minutes' walk from our flat. For days Leon was seen walking up to the church and coming back again. His eyes were red for days, and once I saw a tear coming down his face. He refused to eat, and he died not long after.

Mavros and Leon.

ELENI

On 9 September 1940, I was riding my bicycle through Negrelli Street, the main street of Ismailia, when my brother stopped me and said, "Port Said was bombed last night. Some people were killed; your friend Eleni was one of them."

The memory of my shock at that moment still comes to the foreground when the Second World War is mentioned. Eleni was then seventeen and I was nineteen years old.

Eleni's Greek family and mine had lived for three years in the two flats which occupied the whole of the first floor of a two-storey building in Market Street, Port Said. We each had a balcony that ran along the side and round to the middle of the front of this block of four flats. The ground floor was occupied entirely by a large grocery shop. The balconies of the two flats on each floor were separated by a tall wooden panel. That did not stop us (Eleni and me) standing on either side and talking for hours at a time in the evenings after we had done our homework. We went to the same Greek school, which I completed just before the war started.

I would have never believed that there is a special delight in living in a market street if I had not had that experience. It was, of course, very noisy, but that was irrelevant compared to the pleasure that I derived just from watching people from above, going and coming. The long street was brightly lit up, the boxes of fruit and vegetables were neatly placed next to one another outside the little shops and the sellers called loudly to shoppers passing by.

On the balcony next to Eleni's flat.

There was a greengrocer just opposite our building. I watched him in the evenings dipping his lettuces one by one in a bucket of clean water and shaking most of the water out of them before packing them neatly in a tray ready for the next morning. I have given the same treatment to my lettuces for years as soon as they start looking tired and dehydrated.

For some reason my family moved away from that flat some time before the fatal day of the bombing. The reason could have been that my father could no longer afford the rent when his business started being affected by the fall in the number of ships passing through the canal. The shipping of Greek newspapers, magazines and books from Piraeus to Port Said came to a standstill soon after the declaration of war. My father had to close his agency and our family moved to a smaller flat.

Meanwhile I moved to the small town of Ismailia, south of

Port Said, where I was offered employment in the pharmacy which catered for employees of the Suez Canal Company. This pharmacy was run on the principle of the profits being shared by its customers. The dividend was worked out from the amount each customer had spent in the shop, and it was passed on to the customer every six months. While I was busy with the cashier's duties I also had to sort out, at the end of each week, the week's takings in order to work out the customers' dividends. My pay was £3 per week. I had previously earned the same amount monthly while working in a shipping company in Port Said. This increase in pay justified my moving to Ismailia, where I stayed with my uncle's family until my family could join me. I was, by then, the main breadwinner in the family; my sister helped with her dressmaking, and my brother, three years younger than me, worked for the British in an ammunition depot.

My living in another town did not affect my friendship with Eleni, and I knew that all was not well between her and her family after I left Port Said. Her parents did not approve of her boyfriend, whom she met when she was sixteen. He was a well-known and much liked young man, but he was almost twice as old as she was. He owned a shop on the corner of the market street and the main road. The Greek church and school were only a few minutes' walk away. Most schoolchildren passed the shop, and the Greek community bought their stationery and photographic equipment there.

Eleni, a pretty young girl, used to visit the shop until her parents, somehow, found out about her romance, restricted her movements and limited the time that she was away from them. She must have been near to desperation when she smuggled a letter to a friend who posted it to me. It was a cry for help, suggesting that she was planning to run away from home. This letter disturbed me so much that I caught the first train and arrived unexpectedly on her doorstep.

I stood there for a few seconds, listening to what sounded like a loud argument between Eleni and two members of her family. She was sobbing, and I could not hear her words clearly, but it became obvious to me that I had arrived at a bad time. After a few seconds' hesitation, but before I had time to think the matter through, my finger had pressed the doorbell. All went quiet immediately. Was it one, two or five minutes before Eleni's sister opened the door? It seemed a lifetime to me. My heart was pounding away in anticipation of what I might have to face.

The family had enough time to compose themselves. They asked me in, apologising at the same time about my having to come all that way when Eleni was not at home. They were polite to me, but their manner was awkward and they couldn't hide their wish to be left alone again. I was not made to feel unwelcome, but I did not feel welcome either, although our families had lived next door to each other for some years.

That was my last chance to see Eleni, but I left without seeing her. My last memory of her is the sound of her cries on the day of my visit to her parents' house. The first bomb that was dropped on Port Said by an Italian plane killed her father, her brother and her sister's baby. Several people were killed in the other flats. I heard later that Eleni's younger brother had saved his mother by calling her to join him under a table, where he had run for shelter; he was only about six or seven. Eleni's older sister and her youngest one were also saved.

It was rumoured that the bomb was not meant to be dropped on the population. A bakery in the market was baking bread during that night. The pilot of the plane mistook the light of the chimney of the bakery for a ship in the harbour, which was apparently the intended target. Eleni's body was found at the top of the stairs. She had been suffocated by falling debris.

SCHOOLDAYS

Ferdinand de Lesseps was responsible for the construction of the Suez Canal, which took ten years to be completed and was first opened in 1869. On its completion he gave to the Greek community of Port Said a piece of land on which were later built a Greek Orthodox church and the Greek school which I attended for thirteen years. The donation of that gift of land was in recognition of the part Greek emigrants played in the building of the Suez Canal.

With the opportunity of work, many Greeks left behind them the difficulties of life in villages of mountainous Greece for a new life in the 'Land of Plenty', as Egypt had been known. The River Nile provided water while the Suez Canal contributed to the commercial wealth of Egypt.

The Greek Orthodox church at Port Said.

The School of the Greek Community of Port Said, as it was called from the beginning, started as a primary school for boys and girls with a mixed infant class for five year olds. The school provided six years of primary education. I was accepted in the infant class, which was then called 'Half Class', before I was five because I could read; my older sister, aged twelve, had already taught me.

Permission for the school to acquire the status of a 'complete educational institution' for pupils from the ages of five to eighteen was finally granted by the Greek Ministry of Education in Athens in 1938, which was my final year at school. Approval for the school to issue Final School Certificates came in three stages as the Greek population in Port Said kept increasing and more classes were added.

I was lucky enough to join the fourth, fifth and sixth forms of the secondary school just as they had started functioning for the first time. It was quite a treat to enjoy the privileges of the final year three times, which resulted in me being awarded the King Fuad Prize twice – in the fourth and sixth forms. In June 1938, however, after taking final exams in eleven subjects, my sigh of relief was very short-lived. The Ministry of Education in Athens informed my school that the formalities for the approval of the sixth form were not quite complete yet. This made the Final School Certificates not valid. It was decided that the exams would have to be taken again at the Greek school in Suez, where the sixth form had been functioning for some years.

I can still feel the disappointment and the panic I felt at the thought that I had forgotten everything and there was no time for revision. At a strange school, in a strange town, we had to go through the anxiety of sitting important exams for the second time. My Final School Certificate was issued by the authorities of the school for the Greek community of Suez with a mark of 9.11/13, depriving me of the full 10 mark that I was told I had achieved at my first effort and of the pleasure of having my

Final School Certificate issued by my beloved school in Port Said.

My Final School Certificate contains one more anomaly that needs explaining. The school authorities must have been shown my original birth certificate, which gives 1920 as the year of my birth. According to the old calendar, I was born on 28 December 1920, much to the disappointment of my mother, who was worried that that would add a year to my age. It must have been a joy to her when in 1923 the Orthodox Church adopted the Gregorian calendar. Greeks had to add thirteen days to their original dates of birth, which brought me into 1921.

The infant class, which I joined in 1925, had forty children. From the first year of the primary school the boys would move to the first floor of the building, where they would stay for six years. There were separate playgrounds at the front and back of the building.

The secondary school also lasted six years. The classes were mixed and were situated on the first floor. Some children would leave school at the end of the six primary years in order to continue their education at a French school or to start apprenticeships offered by the Suez Canal Company with the hope of working for that organisation in the future. The system worked well as it gave pupils the choice of either following an academic career or learning a trade. Some pupils later joined their family business.

Secondary school uniform, 1935.

There was no compulsory leaving age. Tuition fees were according to the parents' income. The administration of the school was run by a committee of prominent members of the community.

Textbooks were sent by the Greek Government. Each child had his or her own set of books from the age of eight. Parents were expected to pay a sum for the books, which was calculated according to their means. All textbooks and exercise books had to be covered with blue paper. A label at the front bore the name of the pupil, the subject and the year.

Spaghetti was in those days twice as long as it is today and it was wrapped in good-quality blue paper. My mother must have had to buy who knows how many packets of spaghetti to provide me with enough blue paper to cover all my books. We did, however, buy the smart, white, lined labels, which were surrounded with a double blue line.

Homework started from the age of eight. I still remember my first encounter with it. One day at the end of the Greek lesson the teacher asked us to open our reading books and to put a little mark next to a certain line on a given page. She said, "Tomorrow we are going to do dictation." I still wonder whether she explained to us what to do with that line. She probably did so while I was painfully trying to remember the word dictation in order to repeat it to my sister, who in my opinion knew everything.

In the evening I announced to my sister that I had to do dictation the next morning, and I showed her the line. She told me to take a pencil and a sheet of paper and to write what she was going to read. It all ended in tears on my part because I could not understand why she could look at the words while I was not allowed to copy them. I still remember the pride with which for the first time I copied the date from the blackboard on to the top line of the first page of my first writing book. It was '5th of December, 1928'. Was it the day of execution of that first dictation?

There were frequent school reports signed by the teacher and the head teacher, who also added a comment on the general behaviour of the pupil. The report had to be brought back signed by the parent.

Teaching of foreign languages started at the age of eight, and French was taught throughout the school years. In the last year geography was taught entirely in French, and it was the geography of France. During that hour we were not allowed to utter a word in Greek, and the same rule applied from the beginning of the fifteen-minute break on the playground before the lesson. During all that time a coin was passed secretly from one pupil to another who was heard to speak in Greek. Even best friends were not trusted in case they possessed the coin. The last possessor had to return the coin to the teacher and to lose marks as penalty.

English was introduced in the first year of the secondary school, but it was dropped after the third year, when Arabic became compulsory in all the foreign schools in Egypt. Latin was taught in the last two years. The Greek Government had limited the number of languages to three besides Ancient and Modern Greek. Learning Latin was not the most enjoyable experience of my school life. The headmaster, who taught the language, would throw questions at random, on forming a particular case of a verb, at individual pupils. The anticipation was killing me. I could hear my heart thumping as I waited for my name to be called. Two terms still predominate in my mind at the thought of Latin grammar: *supinum* and *gerundium*.

Religious education was considered to be the most important subject, followed by Greek and mathematics. Failing one of these three subjects meant spending the summer holiday revising in order to resit the exam and to be able to move to the next class. If a pupil failed more than one of these three subjects, he or she would have to spend one more year in the same class. This explains why the age of school leavers ranged between eighteen and twenty-one.

There were three different colours of uniform as children progressed through the classes: light blue with three rows of narrow white tape at the edge of the round collar, cuffs and pockets, for the four first years; navy blue with white collar for the two last classes of the primary school; and black with white collar for the secondary years. There were also Sunday uniforms for church and special occasions: blue skirt with white top and blue tie for the primary school; and a navy-blue dress with a pretty checked bow tie for the older girls.

For PE the girls wore white skirts with blue shirts. There was a PE display by the whole school at the end of the year, and it took place at the sports stadium of the city. That was a proud day for the parents and the pupils, who marched through the city to the stadium.

On National Days like 25 March (Independence Day) and 23 April (St George's Day) Scouts, Guides and other children would line up after the church service and march through the main street of Port Said to the Greek Consulate, where the Greek consul would give a speech from the balcony of the building.

In the Guides.

Going to church on Sundays was encouraged. Pupils who missed church would have to bring a note to the teacher on Monday morning giving the reason. I never objected to attending church in my Sunday clothes. I enjoyed meeting my friends afterwards, and I enjoyed the reading of the Gospel and the speech that followed by the Bishop of Port Said, but I used to find tiresome the chanting by the two choristers who stood on either side of the altar and filled in the intervals with what sounded to me like long-drawn-out vowels, repeatedly going up and down the musical scales. A few pews were the property of some people and a few chairs were reserved for older people, but most of the congregation stood throughout the service.

On special occasions the church would look magnificent, with its gold-framed icons, the tall gold candlesticks and the Bishop's and priests' silk vestments embroidered with gold thread. At the end of the service three young altar boys, one carrying a cross and two carrying tall, white, lit candles would walk down the aisle in front of the two priests, one of whom swung a censer attached to a long chain and the other held a bunch of basil dipped in holy water and sprayed the people standing on either side of the aisle.

A painting on the inside of the round dome of the church often kept me, as a young child, wondering whether God, floating in the air with his cherubs around him, was really watching me. It was an imposing painting with a beautiful sky-blue background. I heard later that the artist had used photographs of some eminent people when they were babies for the faces of the cherubs.

My school years ended just as the war started, so a scholarship to read classics at Athens University never materialised for me. My father's business closed down when the Suez Canal was closed to all traffic. The newspapers stopped coming from Greece and my father found himself unemployed, without a pension or any assistance from the firm he had worked for for twenty years.

When my mother asked him, "What are we going to do now?" he answered, "May God keep my children well."

All of a sudden I had become the main breadwinner of the family. My brother was only fifteen years old.

MY GRANDMOTHER'S ORDEAL

My maternal grandmother died in Egypt in 1933 aged sixty-five. She was Greek but had lived almost all her life in Asia Minor, which is the western part of Turkey and has its coast on the Aegean Sea.

My earliest recollection of my *yaya* – as Greek children call their grandmother – is of her sitting on a stool, with me sitting on a mat beside her, with my head resting on her lap and her apron pulled over my face. Her fingers moving gently through my hair were having on me the mesmerising effect that my mother's lullabies must have had not many years earlier.

Another early memory that I can almost still taste in my mouth is of my *yaya* grinding peanuts in her heavy, brass pestle and mortar, mixing sugar with the powdered peanuts and passing me little spoonfuls of the mixture. The pestle and mortar, together with her two jam pots, her two brass candlesticks, and her censer with the domed lid and the cross at the top travelled with my mother to every country she went to during her unsettled life.

A very distant memory I have of my grandmother is of her being very ill, on a bed which had been moved to the middle of her room. It must have been in the 1920s. I remember someone placing on the side of her forehead what looked to me like a flat worm. I was watching the worm getting gradually fatter, when an adult came and took me away. I learned later that at that time one way of lowering a patient's blood pressure was by allowing leeches – a species of blood-sucking worm – to extract blood from a patient. I do not remember having any feeling at all about it. 'It is just another thing that grown-ups do,' I must have thought.

I was twelve when my *yaya* died. I had never seen her dressed in any colour other than black – as widows did at that time for the rest of their life. Her whole outfit consisted of a long-sleeved jacket buttoned at the front, an ankle-length skirt with an apron tied at the back, and a headscarf folded into a triangle, which covered much of her forehead and was tied under her chin. She was a quiet, dignified figure with a rather sad, thoughtful expression in her eyes. How I wish I had asked her to tell me all about her past!

The history lessons during my Greek primary-school years were based mainly, at first, on Homer's *Odyssey* and the *Iliad*, on the Persian Wars and on the Greek gods. All those ancient stories can keep a child's imagination asking for more; the difference between myth and reality means little or nothing to the listening child.

By the time we were nine or ten, our history lessons had begun to concentrate on the 500 years of Turkish occupation of Greece. We learned about the determination of the Greeks to preserve their religion and language in secret underground churches and schools in continuous fear of persecution by the Turks. These stories fuelled our imaginations, and instilled in us a pride and love for our country.

During the secondary-school years we were taught about classical Greece, including the great Greek philosophers and politicians, as well as nineteenth-century events in Europe. The First World War had ended only a few years earlier. The history of that war had not yet been written, and many of the people who lived through it preferred not to talk to their families about their devastating experiences.

My grandmother's life had already been devastated by wars that had been going on around her country since long before the First World War. These wars were caused by unrest among the Balkan countries, who were fighting for territory with a sea coast. This unrest of smaller countries situated north of Greece was causing rivalry among the stronger and richer countries, especially Austria and Russia, who were for ever reorganising the Balkan States to suit their own interests. Smyrna, the capital of Asia Minor, suffered destruction repeatedly by the armies of the surrounding countries.

At the beginning of the twentieth century the Balkan States took advantage of the rivalry among the stronger countries. They decided to forget their own differences and form a coalition with the aim of freeing Europe from Turkish domination. The two wars between 1912 and 1914, the Balkan Wars, proved to be a disaster for Greeks who lived in Smyrna under Turkish rule and collaborated with the mainland Greeks. They were cruelly punished by the Turks. Thousands of them were forced to leave their homes and seek refuge in Greece and other countries.

My grandmother's brassware and silver jam pots.

During that time my grandmother saw her family disintegrating, and her home was lost to her for ever. One of her sons died from TB in a military hospital while serving with the Greek Army. On a small scrap of paper, which has come into my possession together with some other documents, are his military number and the numbers of his regiment, unit and barracks. Perhaps it was written by him before he died.

When the Greeks left Asia Minor after the Balkan Wars, my grandmother, a widow by then, and her youngest son found themselves as refugees at Thessaloniki, a town in the north of Greece. Her husband had been killed by the Turks. Two daughters went to Egypt, two sons and a daughter escaped to Greece and from there to France, and another daughter went to Crete. There were originally thirteen children, but by that time only seven were living. I have heard that one of the daughters was very beautiful, and in order to avoid the attentions of Turkish soldiers she dressed as an old woman with her face covered up to the eyes. She was told not to say a word, pretending that she was dumb and deaf.

Another story says that the family gathered all their valuable possessions, dug a deep hole near a tree and buried them, hoping that one day they would come back to retrieve them. The two sons and a daughter had spent five years working hard at a factory and saving money hoping to go back home one day. They escaped to France with the new wife and baby of one of the sons. By the end of the First World War conditions in the Balkan countries had become more settled and thousands of refugees had started going back to their homes in Asia Minor. This was also the dream of my grandmother's children – to be with their mother again after having been away for over five years and to start a new life with their family in their old home at their little town near Smyrna. It was not to be. In his last letter from France, one of the sons wrote to his mother that it was only a matter of days before they would meet again as he, his sister and his brother, sister-in-law and baby were waiting for the boat that would bring them from France to Greece. On the night of 15 January 1919 their ship collided with a sea mine near Malta, on the way to Greece. Their mother never saw them again.

My grandmother and her four surviving children: Antony, top left; Anna (my mother) and Irene, top right; and Despina, left.

THE UNBEARABLE LOSS

I have always known that there had been a very tragic event in my maternal grandmother's life during which some of her children had lost their lives. I was twelve when she died and I was told very few details. I remember that every year on All Souls' Day there was a ritual in our house in memory of her dead children. I can see her now sitting in front of a table on which there was a large dish full of what is known by all Greeks as *colliva*. It is made from boiled wheat mixed with cinnamon, syrup, mixed ground nuts and raisins. The surface is made even and it is covered with icing sugar, just as is done with cakes. The similarity, however, stops there. The top is decorated with sugared almonds and tiny silver sweets in the shape of a cross. It is a votive offering from the relatives of the deceased. The dish is taken to the church, where it is placed with dishes prepared by other people. At the end of the normal service the priest calls the names of the dead from a list that the relatives have provided and reads a blessing. The *colliva* is then distributed in small amounts wrapped in paper napkins to members of the congregation. When they have returned home the adults say, "May they rest in peace," and they eat a spoonful. The children just enjoy the delicious-tasting treat.

My grandmother's votive dish was in memory of five members of her family. The details of their death came to me in the 1980s in a bundle of documents which had been in the possession of her youngest son in Australia. A number of letters were written by one of her sons, who with his brother and sister had spent five years in France as refugees after the Balkan Wars. From the content of these letters it appears that they sent money regularly to their mother, but she did not always receive it. In one of these letters one of the sons suggests that they all went to Egypt, where my parents and one of the sisters were already, but he expresses a fear that their ship might collide with a sea mine while crossing the Mediterranean Sea as hardly one year had passed since the end of the First World War. In another letter he is wondering whether everyone could come to live in France, but he says it would be very difficult to obtain visas. My grandmother was then with some members of her family at Thessaloniki as refugees from Asia Minor after the Balkan Wars.

In his last letter, dated 7 January 1919, the son asks his mother not to send any more letters to his address in France because they had left and were waiting in Marseilles for the boat to take them to Greece. He mentions how excited they were at the thought of seeing them again. He finishes his letter with the words 'and God willing may we all meet again at home'. The ship never arrived in Greece. According to information received through the Internet, the passenger ship they boarded at Marseilles was called *Chaouia* and had accommodation for sixty-four first-class and thirty-four second-class passengers. Originally it was the Dutch ship *Koningin Wilhelmina*, built in Vlissingen in 1895. In 1911 it was sold to a Moroccan/Armenian company and it was renamed *Chaouia*. On 15 January 1919 the ship struck a mine and sank in the Strait of Messina.

Among the documents my uncle kept until he died there is one from the Greek Ministry of Foreign Affairs which gives the date of the sinking of the ship as 2/3 January 1919. This date is wrong as the son was still in Marseilles on the 7th. The date of the sinking of the ship was 15 January 1919.

The Chaouia.
(By courtesy of www.stegro.nl)

Constantine (sitting), who died from TB, and Nicolas, who drowned.

John and Madelene who drowned.

The document from the Greek Ministry of Foreign Affairs was written three and a half years after the disaster and it was concerned with the amount of compensation they were prepared to pay to my grandmother. They were offering her either dr.150 per month for life as long as she remained a widow, or the set sum of dr.9,000. They were also offering her dr.5,000 for the lost belongings of the deceased and another dr.5,000 towards the financial loss of their heirs resulting from their death. She had lost in one go two sons, a daughter, the wife of one of the sons and their baby boy.

My grandmother waited and waited for her children to come to Thessaloniki. No one dared to tell her the tragic news. She was made to think that the ship was delayed. Eventually it was no longer possible to hide from her the truth. She said that the previous night she had had a very strange dream. She dreamed that she could hear the cries of her children saying, "Our head is hurting from hitting the rocks."

Granny and her family never returned to their home. My father brought her and her youngest son to Egypt, where she spent the rest of her life.

A LIFELONG SECRET

As the disputes between the Balkan countries continued to go on after the First World War, the Greeks of Asia Minor found themselves persecuted by the Turks for the second time in ten years. The first persecution was after the Balkan Wars because they had collaborated with Greece. By 1919 relations between Greece and Turkey were improving, and many Greeks who had left Asia Minor came back to their hometowns.

In 1919 Greece captured Smyrna from the Turks, and after that the situation continued to deteriorate. In 1922 the Turks recaptured Smyrna from Greece and burned the city. What followed amounted to genocide and has been known since as the Great Catastrophy. The Greeks were ordered to abandon their houses; the men were taken away never to be seen again, or they were killed in front of their families.

Thousands of women and children formed long processions, miles long, and walked from morning to night towards the coast, hoping to be picked up by ships. In many cases the ships never arrived. Desperate people were jumping in any small boats that were available. Children were separated from their mothers, and bundles of belongings that had been carried during all the time of the long walks were thrown into the sea to make more space for people. People spoke later of seeing women and children falling into the water in their attempts to board the overcrowded boats.

Some ships that had been sent by countries to save their

own people refused to take anyone of another nationality. Some men belonging to the crews of these ships were seen pushing back into the water people trying to climb aboard.

My childhood school friend was a baby when her father was taken away. Her mother, with her in her arms, and her ten-year-old sister were forced to leave their house. Her sister remembered her mother stopping suddenly shortly after they left and saying to her, "Stay here. Don't move until I come back." She placed the baby in her arms and walked away. The two children waited only for a few minutes, and the mother reappeared with a small bundle in her hand. The three of them were eventually brought to Egypt.

The family had a jewellery shop in Asia Minor. That small piece of luggage was a lifesaver for them. It was some time before they found, through the Red Cross, the only relative they had. The brother of my friend's mother had been studying in Europe and had had no news from them since they left home. The older sister remembered the first minutes after they met their uncle. When he heard that their father had been killed, he knelt down as if to pray and promised to look after his sister and her little girls throughout his life.

The refugee of Asia Minor.

Some details about that cruel never-ending walk towards the coast by thousands of women and children were given to me by a cousin whose grandmother joined those desperate, hungry, tired people.

My mother's brother came to Egypt with his mother after spending the years of the First World War in Greece. They were refugees from Asia Minor after the Balkan Wars. Later he met his wife, who was also a refugee from Asia Minor after the 1922 second persecution by the Turks. I remember their wedding day in 1927. I thought that that was my day as much as it was the bride's day. I remember dancing the Charleston in a room full of dancing couples at my parents' house after the wedding. I was five years old and I felt all the time that all eyes were on me. Dancing in a room to a gramophone record, after rolling up the mats or carpet, was done with any excuse. I remember women friends of my mother, who also came from Asia Minor, performing beautiful Turkish dances. Families visited one another and they entertained themselves at very little expense. Women had time to embroider and to make lace; men had to do the DIY jobs; and children entertained themselves with very few toys, which they looked after and treasured.

I loved that auntie more than any of the others. Our families always managed to live in the same town and often in flats in the same building, probably because of my mother's love for her mother and her youngest brother and also my father's wish to help and protect the young man who was deprived of his father when he was a little boy. His father was killed by the Turks, two brothers and a sister were drowned, and the rest of the family were living wherever the aftermath of the troubles of Asia Minor had brought them.

My uncle and his young wife were both eighteen when they were married in Port Said. I always had the feeling that something was worrying my young auntie. I remember very faintly that once she had to be taken to the hospital. I found out later that she had had a breakdown, but she was back soon feeling well again. I never knew why she had reached that point of anxiety until recently, when my cousin, her second daughter, told me her secret story.

One day, shortly before she died, my auntie said to her daughter, "There is something that I have wanted to tell you for years." The following is the story as my cousin told it to me on the phone from Australia.

My auntie was only seven years old when her father was killed after a dispute with a Turk at his work. His wife was left with five young children to bring up on her own. It was in the middle of the First World War. She had to take people's laundry in and also to work in the fields for the Turks. People were short of food at that time and she had very little to feed her five children.

One day before she left for work she told her daughter to watch the baby who was asleep, and to give him a piece of bread when he woke up. The seven-year-old girl went out to play and forgot all about the feeding of the baby. This cannot have been the cause of the death of the three-year-old boy, even though many children were dying from malnutrition at the time. However, the little girl grew up with the belief that she had been the cause of her little brother's death.

What really caused the little sister to grow up with such a tormenting conscience was that she remembered that after the baby's death she danced with pleasure at the thought that there would be more bread for her now. Her breakdown was probably the result of her secretly blaming herself for so many years.

My auntie's mother lost one more child before she joined the queues of refugees in 1922. She had to leave with her remaining three children. Together with thousands of other women and children they walked from towns in Asia Minor, much further from the coast than Smyrna, from morning to evening. Then they were given a loaf of bread and a bucket of water for each family to last until the next evening. Two of her children died on the way and she had to dig their graves with her hands and bury them herself. She was left with only the little girl who married my uncle when they were both eighteen.

The old lady outlived her daughter; she lived to be ninety-seven, but never overcame the loss of her husband and her four children in such a cruel way. She became blind in her last years, but her mind remained clear to the end. One night, when she was staying with the granddaughter who told me the story, she got up, gathered all her bedcovers and arranged them on the floor as if she was covering people who were sleeping under them. Then she went back to the bare mattress.

My cousin who had woken up in the meantime went to her and asked her, "Why did you do that, Granny?"

She answered, "The children were cold and I covered them up."

In the morning she did not remember anything about the episode. When her granddaughter told her what she had done in the night she just laughed and said, "Did I? I must be going mad." And she added, "God took away from me four children, but He gave me four grandchildren."

When she died she was the oldest of five generations in her family.

Five generations.

THE LOST COUSIN GEORGE

When my father died in 1942 he was seventy years old and I was twenty-two. It had never occurred to me, up to then, to ask him how he found himself in Egypt. I knew that he was born in Greece, that he was a Spartan and that some members of his family were in America. I had seen photographs of two aunties, one uncle and some cousins in a family album and had presumed that there had been an exchange of letters at some time.

As a child I had never missed those relatives because there were aunties and cousins on my mother's side of the family. I had known and loved them throughout my pre-war years.

After the Second World War my life had completely changed. I was married and living abroad with my own family. As an army wife I was prepared to make the best of a life which offered comfort and financial security as well as unexpected changes and temporary friendships, but no relatives.

That was the time when I most missed having relatives around me. I kept in touch with the ones I knew, but at the same time I was developing a strong longing to find out what had happened to the relatives in America and if there were any still living in my father's village in the Peloponnese.

When the army career of my husband was ended by an unexpected diabetic blackout in the early sixties the change from army life to civilian was not easy with three children aged fourteen, twelve and two. At last in 1973 I was able to consider a visit to Greece with my thirteen-year-old son. I was hoping to trace my paternal roots during a two-week stay there.

We travelled to Athens by coach and spent the night at a hotel, and the next morning I bought two tickets to Tripoli at the railway station in Athens. I felt apprehensive and at the same time excited. Tripoli – I did not know that another Tripoli existed besides the capital of Libya.

This Tripoli was the terminal stop of our train. I was told at the ticket office that coaches and trains went from there to all destinations. They, for some reason, did not supply return tickets; but as I had no idea about the length of our stay at the village, that was no problem.

The Peloponnese is a peninsula at the southern part of mainland Greece. It has been separated from the mainland by the Corinth Canal. Crossing the canal by train was an unforgettable experience. The train reduced its speed to crawling pace while crossing the canal over a bridge at the narrowest point. The Corinth Canal is referred to as one of the wonders of modern times. Looking down through the train window, I tried to judge the distance to the water by the size of the ships that pass through the canal. A ship was there at the time – it looked like a toy. The length of the Corinth Canal is about eighty miles. The imposing height of the walls on either side of the water gives some idea of the enormity of the task of building it. The Corinth Canal crosses the Isthmus of Corinth.

Once over the bridge the train stopped for a while at the town of Corinth, near where the ancient open-air theatre of Epidaurus is situated. But we had to carry on on our way to Tripoli.

Argos, the next town we passed through, was such a beautiful sight! It felt as if we were facing this time a wonder of nature – very green with delightful views – in contrast with the dry, stony environment that we had experienced up till then. From Argos the mythological heroes Jason and the Argonauts set sail in search of the Golden Fleece.

When we arrived at the station in Tripoli little did we know that the next part of our journey would be the hardest. I took for granted that we would be able to jump off the train and on to a coach to carry on our journey. Outside the station we were confronted with taxi drivers, each trying to persuade us that his taxi was the best.

I asked one of them, "How does one get from here to Georghitsi?" That is the name of the village where my father was born. "Is there a coach?" I asked.

"Yes," he replied, "at six in the morning."

Rather than finding a hotel for the night, I decided that the best way to carry on was by taxi. I asked the driver who was standing nearest to me how far away the village was.

"Can you see that mountain not far away? The village is on the other side of it."

We sat in his taxi, believing that we were only a short ride from our destination.

After a short while I noticed that the view kept repeating itself, as if we were going round in circles. We kept facing what we had seen before. This happened time after time. The scenery repeated itself at regular intervals. I felt as if we were going two miles forward and one mile backward. The journey seemed to be never-ending. I could see that we were climbing higher and higher on the mountain. From where I was sitting, next to the right-side window, besides following the puzzle of the scenery I also kept an eye on the proximity of the precipice on our right, fearing that there was not enough space on our left for an oncoming vehicle to pass us.

As time was passing a new anxiety succeeded in overtaking the others. In a panic I asked the driver how much longer the journey would take, and I confided to him that my Greek money would not be enough to cover the fare.

He happened to be one of the most understanding taxi drivers I had ever come across. He asked, "What money do you have?"

I said, "Traveller's cheques," and very reluctantly I added, "and one English £5 note."

I thought that, besides the fact that it was such a small amount, English money would be of no more use to him than traveller's cheques.

He thought for a few seconds and then he said, "Give me the £5 note, and on the way back I shall take you to the bank in Tripoli to change your cheques."

My immediate thought was, 'At least our lift back to Tripoli is secured.'

What a relief that was! I would have needed the Greek money I had if there were no relatives to be found and we had to spend the night at a hotel.

Eventually we arrived at the village and stopped in the main square. It was a very quiet late afternoon – the time when shops normally reopen after the afternoon siesta. The taxi driver walked with us to a small café, and the next few minutes were something between a bad dream and a pantomime. I asked the owner of the café if there was a hotel or a boarding house that catered for bed and breakfast. I had decided to leave the search for relatives until the next day. He looked as if he thought I was speaking in an alien language. He just said no to every question I could think to ask him.

Meanwhile the taxi driver was getting quite agitated. He had taken us, by then, under his wing. All of a sudden the voice of the taxi driver went up to match his temper: "Are you trying to tell us that these people who came from the other end of the world to find relatives will have to go back because there is nowhere for them to spend the night?" he shouted.

The penny dropped for the owner of the café, who in turn had to raise his voice to be heard. The taxi driver was now expressing his objection to the lack of the well-known Greek hospitality.

"What name are you looking for?" he asked me.

When he heard my paternal Greek name he ran to the shop door with his arm stretched out and pointed at a white house at the side of the square, a few steps away. The house was shaped like a cube, with pretty, square windows and a verandah above the entrance.

"There it is!" he said triumphantly. "The whole family of that name are here on holiday."

The taxi driver did not waste a second; he ran over to the house, and in a few minutes he came out accompanied by a man who appeared to be in his middle forties. By that time the little cafés around the square had started opening for the evening. There were customers sitting at the tables, sipping their Greek coffee from tiny coffee cups and rearranging their strings of worry beads with a dexterity acquired by many years of practice.

The man approached me and my son and introduced himself to us. We shared the same surname. I could hear my heart beating so fast! The taxi driver had already told him who I was and why I had come to the village.

Without any delay he took us to a table nearby and said, "Please wait a few minutes; I am going to bring my father."

About five minutes later he came back, walking slowly, next to a tall, slim, smart gentleman, dressed in his black Sunday suit. He appeared to me to be in his late eighties. He had already worked out in his mind that he was a first cousin of my father.

The old gentleman sat down at the table; there were tears running down his face. He kept repeating, "Cousin George – the daughter of Cousin George! We lost him many years ago."

By that time we were all crying, including the taxi driver, who had also taken a seat at the table. I noticed that even a person sitting at the nearest table was wiping his eyes.

Happy at last, knowing that he was leaving us in good hands, the taxi driver whispered to me, "I shall be coming back to collect you tomorrow morning," and he left.

The old cousin after getting over his initial surprise invited us to his house to meet his family. There was his son, whom we had already met, with his young wife and baby daughter, and two daughters with their husbands – eight people in all, looking very puzzled, not knowing how to take us. They had never heard of my father, who had left the village when their father was a young boy. We all felt slightly awkward. They were probably wondering where they could squeeze two more beds, and I was realising by their numbers that the house was already full.

After a while the son came up with a solution of the overnight-stay problem. He said to me, "There is a first cousin of yours just round the corner. I shall take you to meet her."

I felt so relieved that these good people would not have to worry about where we would spend the night. At the same time I could not wait to meet a first cousin. I knew that my father had one brother and one sister. Whose family was I going to meet next?

We walked for some minutes; I lost all sense of direction because by then it was dark and there were very few street lights. We soon stopped in front of a house which I had seen on our way to the village in the taxi. The house was blocking the way to the village, and we were now standing in front of it.

We went up some rickety, almost collapsing, stairs and knocked at the door. A very thin woman in a black dress, with a friendly smile, asked us in. After the cousin explained to her, in a few words, who we were he left. She did not look very surprised; I guessed that the cousin had slipped away and visited her while I was talking with his father and sisters. Her father was my father's brother. The house, which she had lived in since she was married, was her husband's paternal house.

We entered a big room which was parted into two by the fact that one half was at a higher level than the other half. In the higher part of the room were two single beds and a small table on which were standing two icons. There was also a large old linen box. On one of the walls were some hooks, from which some clothes were hanging. The other half of the room contained a table and four chairs and little else besides. The wooden floor was spotlessly clean, as was everything else.

We sat and talked for some time. The woman told me that her husband had been an invalid and unable to work since their children were very small. It was left to her to work and bring them up. Later I asked if I could have a wash before going to bed. She showed me a door and said that I would have to go outside. She gave me a soft, clean towel and I walked out on to a verandah. All that I could see there under the moon and the stars was a tap on the wall.

'A wash in the open air?' I thought, and I looked around; there was no other house to be seen, just mountains grey and bare. No overlooking! I looked down from the verandah and, for the first time in my life, I was standing on the edge of an abyss. Only the verandah railings separated me from it. The village was perched on the side of the mountain, very near to the top. The cool water was welcome after travelling on that hot day of August.

The mystery of facing the same view again and again on our way to the village was solved. The road was zigzagging up the side of the mountain, gaining height very gradually. The mountain was too steep to entertain any other way of ascending it. There were five mountains standing next to one another, forming a circle. The one I was visiting was the only one which had a natural stream running down almost from its highest point.

In the morning, after a good sleep in comfortable beds, we were ready to explore the village. My cousin took us to the edge of the road and showed us how far down she had to ride on a mule to reach the family land which she had been cultivating for years. I could not see the bottom – it was further down than I could see. She grew fruit and vegetables, but her main produce was olive oil from her olive trees. The olives had to be gathered at the right time and taken to the factory which produced and prepared the oil for sale. She had to have help after her three children grew up. They had emigrated to Australia to make a life for themselves – hard perhaps, but more comfortable than the life that their parents' business could offer them at the village.

Before we left the village I asked the cousin to show us my grandparents' home. I had been longing to see the house where my father was born and the garden in which he played as a child. My plea to see photographs of my grandparents was answered with "They are at the bottom of that trunk – difficult to get to them." She obviously did not realise how important that was to me. She did take us to the family house, but we only saw the front verandah. She insisted that it was in too bad a state to show us the inside. I realised later that she had a sister who had made her home there.

Between two cousins at the house that blocked the way into the village.

Later I was told that, unless there is a will, the paternal house traditionally goes to the firstborn son. I heard afterwards that many families in Greece were apprehensive when a long-lost relative appeared suddenly out of the blue. There have probably been cases where children of lost cousins came back to claim their grandparents' estate. Nothing was further away than that from my mind.

My cousin walked us back to the house of the relatives we met the day before because the taxi driver was to pick us up there later in the morning. The reception was very warm and loving this time. They pleaded with us to stay with them for the night and to leave the next day. After the original shock of the day before, they had somehow found a way to squeeze another two beds for us into their home, but we did have to get to Tripoli before the bank closed and it was Sunday the next day.

There was just enough time for me to sit next to the old uncle with a pencil and a notebook, scribbling as fast as I could the names he was quietly giving me. When we came back to England I sorted them out to the best of my ability and managed to compile a rather incomplete family tree – so precious to me. I was hoping to see him again so that I could fill in the gaps, but unfortunately he died at the age of ninety-two, not long after I left. When I visited the village for the second time, it was too late.

We arrived at the bank in Tripoli just as an employee was going to close the door for the rest of the afternoon. Our vigilant taxi driver, who had taken us again under his wing, promptly put his foot in the way and stopped the door closing, while I explained to the assistant the urgency of my case. I must have sounded desperate – he let me in.

In Greece one drives on the right side of the road. We had climbed the mountain the day before at the edge of the winding road, with cars appearing unexpectedly from around the bend in front of us. On the way back I was relieved that we were not going through that frightening experience again.

My young son had taken it all in without complaining. He had learned enough Greek from my mother, who had been living with us for some years since he was born. At the house of the old cousin he happened to be sitting next to one of his daughters. They all remarked how strong the resemblance was between them. I left the village with a leaf that a horse chestnut tree had shed in my grandparents' garden. Did my father ever climb that tree as a young boy? I have dried it and have kept it until now. I wonder how much of the adventure my son will remember when he reads this story.

The uncle in front of his house.

THE FORBIDDEN STONES

In 1972 I visited Greece for the very first time, after having spent twenty-four years in Egypt (where I was born) followed by several years abroad and ten years in England.

Greece for me was the land of Homer, of Hercules and his labours, of the twelve Olympian gods, of the ancient drama, of the philosophers, of democracy, of 500 years under the Turks and of stories of bravery leading to the Greek Revolution of 1821. It was the Greece of schoolbooks, where language, history and religion were the necessary ingredients for the formation of national identity and pride.

These ideals, which are precious to any nation, were preserved by the Greeks in secret schools and churches (often in underground caves) throughout the 500 years of Turkish occupation. Every year, 25 March, a National Day of Greece, is celebrated as the anniversary of the country's liberation from the Turks.

All my idealistic memories, however, did not come to the fore when I arrived at the old airport in Athens and stepped out of the plane into a heatwave of 45 degrees. My first real impressions were of hearing Greek spoken all around me, shopping in Greek shops, meeting Greek relatives and missing the bus – it was still before queuing-up took the place of first come first served – it has all changed since.

I had been told that entry to the National Museum was free. After queuing up once and reaching the front I was asked for my identity card. I offered to buy a ticket, but when they realised that I was a visitor they let me go through – Greek hospitality had prevailed. Identity cards are a way of life in Greece; the photograph on them is enough proof of identification.

My first visit to the Acropolis was almost a disaster. The relatives with whom I went to see the Parthenon decided that it would be less strenuous to climb the hill from the other side, where there was a short cut. One of the relatives was asthmatic. As we were walking towards the Parthenon I noticed that many fragments of pottery were strewn on the ground. My thoughts were confused. 'How can there be so many pieces still left after the millions of people that must have visited the site throughout the years? They must be fake!' I thought. 'But, there again, they do look old.'

Short cut to the Parthenon.

The forbidden stones.

I kept picking up pieces and placing them in a plastic bag out of which I had first removed a sandwich. I was teaching in those days, and I intended to take the fragments back for a project on Greece with my class.

I had been collecting things since the day I arrived, from cards, tickets, wrappers, seashells and stones to insects dried up by the heat.

Suddenly a man's voice came over a loudspeaker: "Drop that down immediately!" said the voice.

I had just picked up a piece of pottery and was staring at it, admiring the pretty design on it – I dropped it very fast out of my hand. Now I had a dilemma: should I empty the bag too?

I decided to keep a few stones. On our way out, through the main exit this time, the first thing that was staring at me was a giant noticeboard warning people that they would be prosecuted if they picked up stones or fragments from the ground. There was no such warning at the other entrance.

I cannot help making comparisons between countries. I remember thinking that there were as many pastry shops there as there were fish-and-chip shops in England, and perhaps as many churches there as there were pubs here. Shops closed at 1 p.m., leaving the hot afternoons free for a siesta at home. Schools were open from 9 a.m. to 2 p.m.

Wherever one went, even in poorer districts, one would see large notices on balconies advertising private tuition in languages at all levels, with English predominating. Parents were very involved in their children's education and interested in their progress at school. University places were fewer than the number of applicants for further and higher education. Private lessons, not only in foreign languages but also in Greek, mathematics and many other subjects, were part of a child's education from a very early age. I noticed that school homework and extra private tuition left the children with very little time for reading for pleasure. Private lessons were in many cases carried on throughout the summer.

Another thing that became very obvious to me as soon as I reached the outskirts of Athens was the amount of building which was going on everywhere. Some houses were in the process of being built, but the sites looked abandoned, with no workers to be seen anywhere near them. I found that these houses belonged to people who were paying for building work as the money became available. Sometimes they would put the building on hold for years, until they had saved enough money for the next stage of building, and so on. Many had found work in Australia or America, where there were higher wages, and they sent money back to relatives to carry on with the building.

Passing on property to their children is a major preoccupation of Greek parents. Paternal homes are kept from generation to generation. They are used in the summer when members of the family from all over Greece and from abroad gather for a family reunion. My great-aunt was ninety-six in 2006, and she was anxiously waiting for her only son to visit her from America with his family, including two great-grandchildren. He had been to see her himself once or twice a year, but this time he was bringing his whole family to introduce the second great-grandchild to his mother. The old lady was so excited about them coming that they kept the date secret. The son is the only one in his family who speaks Greek. Their paternal home in the village was too far away for his mother to travel to for the gathering, and her flat in Athens was too small to accommodate them all. The son stayed with her and his family stayed at a hotel, which left the old great-grandmother with the feeling that she did not see them enough. She saw her son again in the following three years, and she died just after her 100th birthday.

THE STRANGER ON THE TRAIN

I normally discourage fellow-travellers from unloading their chests and reciting their life stories to me. Such people often end up asking personal questions. I have had one or two experiences on coaches, when, at the end of the journey, I have been left with a headache and I have promised never to step on a coach again.

In the following instance, the fellow-traveller was a man with an American accent.

It happened one day back in the 1980s, while I was travelling by train from Portsmouth to Norwich to spend a few days with my daughter. At one of the stops between Portsmouth and London the carriage door was opened by a man holding a huge suitcase in one hand and a briefcase in the other. He seemed to be having great difficulty in lifting the suitcase over the step. He staggered through the door, stood still for a second or two, looked round the carriage and decided for some reason to come and sit in the vacant seat next to mine.

I remember wondering why he preferred the seat near me rather than the double seats available in the not so crowded carriage. That thought was one of those quick observations which come back to mind at a later date when one tries to make sense of a puzzling mystery.

Well, one can hardly call this story a mystery, but it left me with questions that have remained unanswered. The man was tall, slim, smartly dressed and well spoken – the type that one feels able to trust right from the beginning.

We exchanged a hello, and a few minutes later he opened his briefcase and brought out a photograph album. He opened the album, turned one or two pages over, and attracted my attention to a rather large photograph. It was a picture of three people. They were – he told me – his wife, his eighteen-year-old son and his sixteen-year-old daughter. They were standing in front of a beautiful, large detached house.

Suddenly I noticed that his hands were trembling and he was in tears. He said that a few months earlier he had had a nervous breakdown, so his family had arranged for him to come to this country on a two-week tour to recover.

I was wondering if the best thing his people could have done for him was to send him on his own to the other end of the world. I asked him outright why he was so unhappy.

He answered that on that particular morning a telegram had arrived for him from America. It was sent to the tour representative by his wife's sister. It said that his house had burned down during the night and his wife and children were all dead. He explained that he had abandoned the tour and he was on his way to London to take the first plane back to America.

The thought of his heavy suitcase went through my mind when he said that he had bought a lot of gifts for his family. I could have cried as I imagined him no longer having loved ones to give his presents to. The man went on to point out that he had spent so much on gifts that he did not have enough money left to buy a return air ticket.

I asked him how much money he was short of, and he said, "About £60."

After a short pause I said to him, "I don't have enough money on me, but when we get to London I shall draw some out of the bank for you."

He thanked me and insisted that he would send it back to

me. He passed me a piece of paper and a pen to write down my address; then he wrote his name and address on another piece of paper and gave it to me, insisting all the time that he was only borrowing the money from me.

When we arrived in London we left the train and walked towards the exit of the station. I stopped to ask a passer-by if there was a bank nearby.

He said, "When you get out of the station turn left and walk on. There is a bank not far away from here."

I asked the man I had met on the train if he would mind looking after my luggage and waiting for me there until I came back. I followed the instructions of the passer-by in a panic.

I could not see a bank sign anywhere in the near distance. The thought of missing my train to Norwich, and anxiety about leaving my luggage with a strange person, made me quicken my pace and I almost missed what I was running for. I was beginning to wonder whether the bank was in the opposite direction. Did the passer-by really say "turn left"? I stood still and looked up in desperation – or was it for inspiration? There was the bank sign, above my head. I was standing just outside the entrance of the elusive bank. I entered with a sigh of relief, but the length of the queue of people waiting to be served made my heart sink. I waited for what seemed an eternity. Before I reached the head of the queue I took my chequebook out of my bag and opened it to be ready – every second counted. To my horror there were no cheques left in it. I had used the last one when I had bought my ticket to Norwich one week in advance to save on the fare. I had forgotten to replace in my bag the old chequebook with the new one. I had no time to consider whether to give up and go back to my luggage and face the man with my side of the story or to explain the situation to the assistant and hope for the best.

"Can I help you?" said the voice from behind the screen.

I thought, 'And how!' but I did not know how to start. I just showed her the chequebook and asked if I could speak to the manager. I was embarrassed to explain my mistake with the chequebook knowing that the people in the queue would hear.

The assistant left her desk, asked for someone else to take her position, and indicated to me to follow her to a corner of the room. Very politely she asked me again how she could help me. When she heard that I wanted to draw out some money in order to help out a fellow train passenger who was unknown to me she looked as if she could not believe her ears. Before she could remind me of the risks of trusting a stranger I asked her again if I could speak to the manager.

"Please wait for a few minutes," she said, and she disappeared through a nearby door.

The next few minutes seemed never-ending. Eventually she reappeared and ushered me into an office.

After a friendly handshake, the manager asked, "How can I help you?"

Now it was my turn for a repeat. I was by then determined not to go back to the man at the station only to tell him that I had run out of cheques. During the next few minutes I felt as if I was playing with the manager the then popular game of twenty questions. After giving my name, my maiden name, my father's name, my address, the name and address of my bank, the address of where I was going in Norwich, and so on, the manager asked what felt like the twentieth and was probably the most important question: "Do you have any identification papers with your signature on? A passport? A driving licence?"

"Sorry, no," I answered. "I only have my chequebook with me."

A sudden thought flashed through my mind. I suggested that I would pay for any expenses if he was kind enough to phone my bank manager in Portsmouth and ask for my particulars.

'Why did he not think of that?' I wondered. I was worrying about the wasted time, more than the possibility of him thinking I was trying to advise him on how to do his job.

He took my advice anyway.

While the bank manager was on the phone I was mentally fighting with one vital question: how much shall I ask him for? The sum in my head kept increasing as I considered the man's situation. What if he needs a meal? What if he has to wait until next day for the earliest plane? What if he needs to spend the night in a hotel?

"How much would you like to draw?" The manager's voice stopped the escalation of the sum to be given to the man I had met on the train.

"Oh, £125, please," I hurried to answer.

After filling in a form, signing it and collecting the money, I ran back, wondering for a second whether the man would still be there. When I spotted him, still standing next to two lots of luggage, I experienced a feeling of shame for allowing myself to imagine him walking away carrying my heavy suitcase as well as his own.

All I wanted then was to catch my connection; I had very little time left to get to the next platform.

I placed the money in the man's hand and said to him, "I don't want this money back, but I would like to hear that you arrived safely and that you are well. Have a meal and take a taxi to the airport."

We shook hands while the man kept insisting that he would send the money back to me. I rushed to the next platform and caught the train just as the guard was ready to blow the whistle for the train to depart.

I have never heard from the man since.

My family and friends were very little impressed when I told them about his shaking hands and his tearful eyes. They thought of all the questions that did not enter my mind: Why was he not helped by the tour company? Why did he not contact the American Embassy? Were the name and address he gave me genuine? Who were those beautiful people on the photograph? Why did I not ask to see the telegram from his sister-in-law which brought him the news that his family and his home had perished in a fire during the morning we met on the London train?

Deep in myself I want to believe that he was genuine, and that is the reason why I have not tried to find out. But did the stranger on my train jump on to the next train, and did he sit next to another – perhaps naive – lady again? Who knows? If by any chance he did try again, let us hope that the next Good Samaritan had neither money nor a chequebook on her – run out of cheques or not.

RAFINA AND THE 2004 OLYMPICS

Since 1981 I have been spending part of my summers at Rafina, a small town on the east coast of Greece. Travelling by taxi from the old airport of Athens to my destination became more and more difficult as the years went on. Rafina was developing from a small fishing village to an important link between Athens and the Aegean Islands.

The old road between Athens and Rafina had not shown much change with the passing of time. In the central reservation of the long road at a point approaching Rafina I always looked out for the bronze statue of a young man standing on one foot, in a running position. He is the young man who ran from Marathon to the stadium in Athens over 2,500 years ago. He was the messenger sent by the Greek army to Athens to announce their victory at the Battle of Marathon. Two thousand Athenians, under General Miltiades, in 490 BC, had overcome 100,000 Persians.

The long road which links Athens to Rafina, and carries on to Marathon, is situated roughly on the path that the young runner must have followed. The first modern Olympiad took place in Athens in 1896. When in 2004 the 29th Olympiad came to Athens, the torch-bearers carried the torch along this road, each passing it to the next young man waiting for it at the entrance of the next town. The son of a friend of mine was the torch-bearer of Rafina.

In spite of many difficulties, the preparation for the Olympic

Games was the catalyst for a great change in Athens and in many other locations connected with the games. The underground Metro, the new airport, the stadium, the Olympic Village and the many venues for the games were all completed in good time. On the eve of the games a proud nation was ready to conduct successfully the great international event which had originated on its soil.

At first it was difficult to imagine how everything would be ready in time to welcome the thousands of visitors that would come from the four corners of the world. Life became difficult for the Athenians – especially during the building of the new underground Metro, which would run alongside the Rafina to Athens road. The half-hour's drive by car became a two-hour journey after the year 2000, when the Olympic Games were allocated to Athens. The road to Rafina, because of its connection with Marathon and the Olympic torch, became one of the main projects.

A substantial sum of money given to Greece by the EU had helped the naval authorities of Rafina to expand the port and its business by increasing the number and size of ships travelling to the Aegean Islands. The already overcrowded little town acquired a port which added to its difficulties but did not contribute to its well-being. As the movement at the port increased, visitors to the islands increasingly tended to park their cars in Rafina and collect them on their way back. The small, quiet town of Rafina was in danger of becoming a parking place of hundreds of cars left for whole weekends and even weeks, free of charge, on every available piece of ground and on both sides of its narrow streets. Their owners collected them when they returned and promptly left Rafina behind.

The side roads lost their charm and peace, and the old-fashioned souvenir shops closed because of the lack of customers. The port was becoming too big and too busy for the small town of Rafina, and eventually its rapid expansion came to a stop. There were rumours that part of its business might have to be moved to a more suitable town along the coast.

Using money allocated to Greece by the EU, many other projects were undertaken in the run-up to the Olympic Games. The town of Rafina was restored and became self-sufficient again. New modern shops, revitalised hotels, a children's playground with an open-air café nearby where the parents could sit and watch their children playing, new bank buildings, easier access to Athens, and frequent buses running to and from Venizelos, the new airport and the numerous villages around are some of the improvements that the 2004 Olympic Games brought to Rafina.

The long road between Athens and Rafina is now a pleasure to travel along, and the statue of the Marathon runner is proudly displayed at a more convenient site. There are official car parks, and the parking charges provide Rafina with a good income.

The port of Rafina.

A NATIONAL DISASTER

A satellite picture published in a Greek Sunday paper, on 28 August 2007, was headed 'The Great Catastrophy' and showed the world on fire. On this picture red patches represent small fires and yellow patches represent big fires. Greece was one of the countries devastated by fires that summer, and for eight days in August there was a national emergency. I shall never forget my holiday in Rafina, from where I watched the flames of fires in Evia. On television, the progress of the fires was shown continuously, day and night.

On Friday 24 August, at 11 a.m., a fire was already burning uncontrollably on the north-east coast of the Peloponnese, heading towards inhabited areas. By 11.30 a.m. houses and businesses in the nearest village were burnt out. People were being evacuated from surrounding villages as fast as the flames, aided by strong winds, were chasing them. New fires were breaking out continuously at new spots, and the fire brigade was finding it impossible to cope. At 1 p.m. one fireman dropped dead, overcome by the flames, and by 2 p.m. there were six people dead in one village alone.

The fire was raging, moving from one village to the next, burning extensive areas of beauty and destroying crops. By 5 p.m. the fire had reached the county of Elia and was approaching the town of Zaharo, where there is a lake of medicinal waters and a well-known health resort. The manager, together with four of his staff and 100 visitors, gathered on open ground where there were no trees, near the sea. Soon the wind direction changed and these people realised that they were being surrounded by flames. A wood nearby had caught fire, and their only hope was a jetty, to which they ran. The fire was now raging on both sides of the jetty. They stayed there for about twelve hours, until dawn. Some of the customers of the resort were elderly. They were moved away in dinghies not a moment too soon.

A twelve-mile ring of fire surrounded the town of Zaharo, leaving no way out. On the television we saw fifty people gathered together in the village square. A few women were sitting on chairs; all the others were standing. One of the women was sitting on a chair with a baby on her lap. She kept wiping the baby's face with a damp cloth. The television picture was very dark because of the black smoke that filled the atmosphere. This woman looked so helpless and touching. I tried to take a photograph of the television screen, but it came out very dark, showing very faintly the mother and her child.

Three firemen and nine villagers lost their lives that night. Eight people were found dead in their cars. Water was dropped from helicopters on to the flames, but they could not fly near enough to save the village. The last count showed forty-two dead, nine missing, 400 homes destroyed and 1,000 people homeless. From eighteen villages only two survived. Pictures were published of people who in desperation were approaching the fire, trying to extinguish it with buckets of water or by beating it with branches of trees, endangering their own lives. A farmer, whose sheep were on fire, was beating them gently with a tree branch to save them.

His wife, who was suffering from shock, was heard saying, "In one hour the house will have gone."

A fireman jumped out of a fire engine and ran towards the fire, pulling a hose. People surrounded him, and each person tried to pull him towards his own house, in all directions.

The fireman said to a news reporter who was present, "Five of us go to put out the fire. One is the deputy chief, two are supervisors, one is the driver, and I am the only one with the hose.

Tell me where to start."

That man had not slept for three nights.

A woman was standing in the middle of the ruins of her house as she spoke to a reporter about finding her husband at three o'clock in the morning surrounded by flames. She also mentioned that the man next door was trying to put his seven children in his car while the tyres were beginning to melt from the heat.

An eighty-five-year-old man and his seventy-nine-year-old wife were shown clearing away stones and bricks to put up a temporary home until their house was rebuilt.

"It will all be green again," the man said.

Pictures headed 'National Tragedy' were published in the free paper. The television kept showing a house which refused to fall, standing among the ruins of other buildings.

While fires were menacing the Peloponnese, other fires were also flaring up all over Greece. The east coast of the mainland and the island of Evia were particularly badly hit, and whole districts were burnt out. A beautiful stretch of green land of 10,000 acres with six houses standing on it became a grey, desolate place after two fires swept over it.

The famous ancient site of Olympia was saved from complete destruction almost by a miracle. Its grounds of outstanding natural beauty were destroyed as was the building where many ancient artefacts were stored or kept for repair. The dr.2.5-billion apparatus to fight any fire at up to 65 yards did not operate on that day. Luckily the museum where the famous statue of Hermes is displayed was spared what would have been a disaster not only for Greece but for the whole world. Thousands visit the site annually, mainly to see the statue of Hermes by Praxiteles.

More and more horror stories were published every day. At one village many of the villagers decided not to leave, but one woman thought her five children would be safer if she took them away. Her house was the only one that survived the destruction. Another woman was found with three of her children in her arms and the fourth nearby, overcome by the fire.

A small child at a burnt-out village said to his mother, "I don't want to look. Take me away from here."

In some places people, in their panic, forgot to let animals out of their enclosures when they themselves escaped. Passers-by running for their lives could hear the animals' screams. I watched on the screen a dog running to and fro, not knowing which way to turn. The sunlight was shut out by the smoke, as the flames shot high into the air.

A civilisation thousands of years old, monuments – objects of international admiration – were caged in by flames.

When the fires were at last controlled and people were out of danger the country had to face the aftermath. There were uprooted families to be rehoused, dead people in the streets to be buried, neighbourhoods hundreds of years old to be rebuilt. Someone spoke of 'ashes in the souls and ashes in the taste of people'.

The need for animal food and for young people to return to the villages and to rear livestock again became paramount. Farmers were given only 11 pounds of food per sheep per week. Fences and enclosures needed to be rebuilt.

In some places the fires were followed by flooding.

The most important emergency of all was to make sure that children were helped to overcome post-traumatic stress. A professor of paediatrics, the director of a paediatric clinic, published an article in which he wrote that 30 per cent of children who endure severe stress from events such as fires and traffic accidents experience post-traumatic stress disorder. For some, it can last six months or even longer, and it may be triggered by a sudden memory of the episode. It could affect the child's schoolwork, his family and the whole society in which he lives. The professor said that support is needed from relatives, friends and teachers until the symptoms ease with time. In severe cases help should only be given by experienced health officials.

As was stated in a newspaper article, 'The National Disaster was immeasurable.' This is true in many more ways than the material losses caused by the fires.

NO TOUCH!

To talk about arthritis in general is like believing that a pair of shoes could be made to fit all foot sizes. My arthritis is a personal thing to me – now I feel it, now I don't. Have I read somewhere, or have I heard, that there are 200 types of arthritis? That possibility makes me feel less anxious about it. At least I am not on my own; there must be worse cases than mine.

Until I had arthritis I never thought that the keys on a typewriter could be so stubborn. They seem to change places with the letters either on the right of them or on the left, according to which direction my arthritic joints have turned the tips of my fingers.

The word *debilitating*, which I noticed on a medical form given to me to take from one department to another at the clinic, sums up my arthritis. I would rather not have known the term. How difficult can arthritis make life? Is there a limit to its progress? If not, then perhaps the limit of age is a blessing – but let us not get morbid.

Let us think of the blessings that go with arthritis, especially if one has an overprotective daughter – or should I say *overcaring*? – who sometimes takes it for granted that old age is synonymous with absent-mindedness, poor memory, failing sense of balance and direction, and opening the door to strangers and offering them a cup of tea while their partner in crime enters the bedroom and helps himself to the newly collected pension.

Did I notice you nodding to each one of these examples? Well, you may be right – not in my case, though! I would not admit it to anyone, even if you were right – which you are not. I would not even admit it to myself. Is it not again a case of one shoe fitting all sizes?

I would like to believe that my arthritis is one of the best, if I can use that term, rather than one of the worst types. One no longer has to wind up watches, but I have learned that one still needs one's fingertips to button up clothes, to pull up a zip fastener, to hold and thread a needle, to comb one's hair . . . The list could go on and on.

In spite of having a multitude of gadgets, life is not as automated as we sometimes think. One has to use one's fingers to work the gadgets. And what about arthritis in the leg joints?

This brings me to the overprotective daughter and to my experiences when travelling lately by air. My daughter had bought the tickets, and she had made arrangements concerning my comfort before, during and after the journey. This must have involved a considerable amount of arranging with the people concerned, from the ticket agents to the wheelchair-pushers at both ends of the flight. By the time we stood in front of the appropriate window to give in our luggage all the links in the chain of employees had been informed about my age and disability. Someone was looking out for me; he recognised me – was my age so obvious? – and came to me. He explained that arrangements had been made for me to be picked up at a certain point by a wheelchair-pusher, who would bring me to the appropriate departure gate. We sat, my daughter and I, at a bench near the pickup point and stopped every wheelchair-pusher speeding in any direction. I repeated my name to each one of them, and each time I knew by the blank look on his or her face that some other 'invalid' was waiting for them anxiously at another pickup point. There were probably at least sixty arrival and departure gates, though, hopefully, there were not as many wheelchair users.

I started worrying that I had missed the plane. The flight time had passed and no departure-gate number had yet been displayed on the overhead information board. The wheelchair arrived eventually. It was obvious from the first minute that my wheelchair-pusher was in a great hurry. After he made sure that all of me was in the chair he placed himself behind it and proceeded to walk at the speed of light. My daughter, both hands loaded with the hand luggage, including the rather heavy duty-free carrier, was trying to keep pace with him. I had no time to ask her to let me take a piece of luggage on my knee to lighten her load a little. I kept telling her to slow down, but she was probably afraid that I might be deposited somewhere on another planet, never to see her again; so she carried on running. I asked the man to go a little slower, but I might as well have been addressing myself to a speed maniac.

Exhausted and out of breath after a gigantic effort to approach the 'marathon runner', my daughter touched him with her finger on his arm. She had no time to reassure him that her gesture was only to beg him to slow down. His reaction came out in the words "No touch!" and, having exhausted his limited vocabulary, he carried on running. He soon arrived at the waiting room and rushed through the narrow passage between the two halves of the crowded room. People had one second to pull their legs out of the way. He stopped next to the front row, where a lady was sitting with her hand luggage beside her. How did he persuade her to move away without a word? I did not have time to thank either of them. He flew away as soon as my feet touched the floor. I felt so embarrassed – more because I did not look much of an invalid than for any other reason. Mind you, the never-ending corridors leading to the departure gate would have been too much for me to undertake on foot – and that is between us, of course.

Next minute I saw my wheelchair-pusher dashing in the opposite direction with another passenger, who had just arrived at another arrivals gate three steps away.

We eventually found our seats on the plane, hoping that we would soon be on our way. We had left our home in Cambridge at 11 a.m. to allow ourselves enough time to get to the airport and visit the gift shops.

We had expected to arrive in Athens at 9.30 p.m., but the three-hour delay of our plane, which came from the United States, resulted in our landing at Athens Airport at 12.30 p.m.

The wheelchair-pusher at Athens Airport was a very friendly man, anxious to help, but he was already out of breath when he met us. This was probably because he was so overweight. He looked as if he could do with me pushing him around instead. He asked us for a euro to pay for a luggage trolley, and, after he indicated to the trolley queue that he was helping an invalid, he placed himself in front of the queue. He pushed me in the wheelchair with his right hand and the trolley containing our hand luggage with his left. He refused to let my daughter push the trolley, in spite of the difficulty he was having in trying to keep all the eight wheels under control.

We eventually approached the unloading bay and I was wheeled towards the conveyor belt. Two people made space for me by moving their trolleys behind them. My wheelchair-pusher stood near me, waiting patiently for our luggage to appear. For some time one giant suitcase kept disappearing and reappearing on the circular belt; it had probably been left behind by a passenger of the previous plane, who must have been thinking that it was lost.

A message was transmitted after a few minutes saying that our plane had just started unloading. That gave my helper the opportunity to get something off his chest and ask for my help. He said that he was very worried about his excessive smoking and his inability to stop.

'Eating?' I thought, noticing his non-existent waistline.

Our luggage was loaded on to the trolley and our good helper proceeded again to perform the difficult feat of pushing trolley and wheelchair with one hand on each. My daughter kept pace with him as we passed through the long corridors of the new, beautiful Athens Airport.

When we arrived at the taxi rank outside, I recognised many of my fellow-passengers from the plane. They had formed a queue, which extended as far as I could see. The wheelchair-pusher placed me at the edge of the pavement in front of the queue, and ran to the first waiting taxi just as the people at the head of the queue were moving towards it.

While the taxi driver was placing our luggage in the boot of the car my wheelchair-pusher was still asking me, almost in tears, what he could do to stop himself from dying. He said that he was only forty-seven. He seemed to believe that he already had one and a half feet in the grave. What made him think that I had the solution to his smoking problem? What could I advise him in the two minutes left before I vacated the wheelchair and he closed the taxi door behind me?

All I managed to say to him was "Go and see a doctor and do exactly what he tells you."

At the same time I put in his hand a 10-euro note, hoping that it would not be spent on a big piece of baklava and a glass of ouzo. He could not stop expressing his gratitude – for my advice perhaps? – until the taxi moved away.

Greek taxi drivers are normally friendly and slightly curious to know where you have come from and how long you are staying. But Athens was quiet at that time in the morning and so was our driver. Not a word! Our one attempt at conversation was to ask what kind of weather they had had during the day; he answered in a monosyllabic groan, so we kept quiet until we reached our destination.

I had in my hand 30 euros, hoping that they would more than cover our fare. I had 40 euros to start with, but I had given a 10-euro note to the nice asthmatic man earlier. The rest of our money was at the bottom of my hand luggage.

I nearly fainted when I heard the driver saying, "Thirty-two euros."

Sheepishly I offered him what I had in my hand and said, "I am sorry – I don't have any change."

It was like showing a red cloth to a bull. The man did have a voice after all.

"Is this what you do in England? I have spent six years in England, and I have never come across anything like this."

I did not catch the rest of what he was shouting about. My worry was that he would wake up the neighbours – and especially the two Alsatian guard dogs next door. They had kept quiet so far. All I wanted was to get indoors without any more fuss.

In the meantime my daughter, who had kept silent up to then, said very politely to the driver, "Would you please help us with the luggage?"

For a few seconds I thought that the bull was going to charge at the red cloth – but no. The man picked up the two suitcases, carried them up the seven steps to the verandah and dashed back down to the taxi, still objecting to the loss of the two euros.

I had to ask my daughter, "How did you dare to ask him to help with the luggage?"

She answered, "The meter in the taxi showed only 24 euros. He knew that he was overcharging us."

WHY?
(*Thoughts by a member of the U3A*)

Reading my stories to my Writing Workshop colleagues is one thing and addressing the group on a special occasion, as I was once asked to do, is another. As a member of the U3A for several years now, I have more or less overcome the inhibitions of accent and age that were prominent when I first applied to join for two courses. That is perhaps owing to the feeling of understanding and acceptance that I have experienced with other members of the U3A.

The other day I asked the tutor of my art group, "How do you put up with us?" and she answered with a smile, "I don't know."

I thought, 'I know the answer.' It is because if she was not the exceptionally kind and patient person that she is, she would not have volunteered to undertake the task. She did not realise that before I asked her that question I had heard her whisper to herself, "I teach them one thing and they go away and do the opposite."

That must be exasperating after having explained and demonstrated to us points such as the difference between shadow and tone or the use of perspective in composing a picture.

"You must use your imagination" is another favourite piece of advice of our art tutor. Imagination is the elusive ingredient – you either have it or you do not, and you can use it only if you possess it. Another helpful hint when she catches us carrying on painting with an almost dried-out brush is "You can't paint without water." And to people who don't know when to stop she might say, "Leave it now. Don't go over it again."

I have never asked the Writing Workshop tutor how she puts up with us. Her answer would also probably be "I don't know" as, in a way, tone, shadow and, especially, imagination are also necessary for good writing. The group – of hopeful future published authors – listen to one another's pieces of writing and offer constructive comments with as much tact and objectivity as possible.

One comment by the tutor that I have found most useful is her question "How did you feel, yourself?" It made me realise that that ingredient joins together events into a narrative that otherwise might sound like a tiring and not so exciting list of facts.

What really brings me down to earth is the tutor's question "For whom are you writing?" That makes one wonder: 'Is what was just read of any interest to anyone at all?' Perhaps the answer to the tutor's question is that we write mainly for ourselves, or to fulfil that ambition of becoming one of those authors whose names are familiar to millions of people. But, sadly, for most of us that will remain a wish, just like the watercolour masterpiece which is waiting to come out of the efforts of the painting group.

One possible answer to the 'Why?' question could be that we may wish to share with others what we consider interesting, amusing, didactic or in some way useful in helping the reader to understand his or her own fears, inhibitions or hidden uncertainties. At the same time we ourselves go through the cathartic process of coming to terms with past events that we cannot change.

Autobiographical stories are sometimes a plea for forgiveness for past mistakes, and the writing of them could mark the beginning of living with those mistakes peacefully. If the very act of writing is beneficial, then does it matter whether anyone at all will ever read the stories?

Sometimes reading can be a trip down memory lane. There is a certain pleasure in reading about familiar events, people and places. Readers relive happy or sad parts of their lives, while realising that they are not on their own.

Many of us at the U3A are supposed to be 'retired'. This generally means we are retired from earning – from doing work that we may not have enjoyed doing. What is certain is that one does not have to retire from using one's physical and intellectual abilities. The pleasure of retirement is mainly in doing things that we have never had time to do before, and in doing them in our own time. Things often take a little more effort and time than they would if we were younger.

Our physical and intellectual efforts before retiring from paid work may have helped other people, and after retirement some of us are able to go on helping others, perhaps by giving them a new interest. Unfortunately, for various reasons, not all of us are able to do this. This brings me back to the volunteer tutors, whose efforts encourage us to get out of bed early enough to be at our U3A meetings on time.

The younger ones of us are probably thinking at this minute, 'Speak for yourself, dear!' They are right: what would I do without my U3A course meetings!

JUNK MAIL

What is junk mail? It is the mail one can do without. It is not worth the effort of picking it up from behind the front door. It seems to be a waste of money on the part of those who use it for advertising their goods. Its manufacture adds to pollution and its disposal costs money. There are notices on some front doors saying, 'No Junk Mail, Please', and the unfortunate deliverer has had a wasted walk to another front door. Junk mail is not even worth the energy that the vicious-sounding dog behind the letter box spends in barking at the intruder. It may even cost the unlucky postman a finger.

Well, I am glad there has never been a 'No Junk Mail' notice attached to my front door.

On one particular Wednesday some years ago I had spent some hours shopping. I came back home tired and loaded and I almost tumbled over a pile of papers inside the door. It had been a particularly favourable day for junk mail. Besides the pizza leaflets – and there were several pizza shops competing in the area – there were a free property magazine, a free local paper, free offers from supermarkets, the Avon book, a cleaner's pamphlet, insurance offers, an agent's assurance that I had exactly the right property for their Mr X, leaflets from a plumber and a decorator, and who knows what else! I walked over it all and proceeded to make myself a cup of tea. I emptied my shopping trolley, forgetting all about the junk mail.

I had to face it again, though, when later I went to lock the front door before going to bed.

At first I thought, 'That can wait till tomorrow.' I bent over and was just pushing it into a pile when a very bright-coloured leaflet appeared from underneath. It said, 'What's inside could make you a Lotto millionaire.'

I remember thinking, 'Oh yes – another one of those that win you £25,000 if you ring a certain number.'

Just the same, I left the lot until the next morning, when I looked again at the bright-coloured leaflet. I unfolded it and found attached to it one of those forms that one has to fill in in order to buy a lottery ticket after paying £1 per go. The form had already been filled in with six numbers, which were underlined.

The leaflet explained that on the following Saturday the name 'National Lottery' would be replaced by the name 'Lotto'.

I placed the leaflet on the table and never gave it another thought until Saturday, when I thought, 'I intend to buy a ticket today in any case, so why not use the numbers that are given to me? One never knows!'

I went to the little newspaper shop round the corner, presented the owner with the filled-in form, paid the £1 and left with the lottery ticket.

In the evening, when the winning numbers were being announced on the television, I remember marking the first three numbers as correct. Then when the fourth one was wrong I thought, 'Well, £10 won – better than nothing.' I could not believe my ears when the fifth number was correct, and then the sixth, and, to top it all, the bonus number was also correct. For a few moments I wondered whether I had misheard some of the numbers. When all the winning numbers came on the screen again and I checked them over, I was in no doubt that I had a winning ticket.

The feeling of panic that I felt at first took a few minutes to subside. I had to tell somebody. I phoned my daughter, but she was not in. Next I phoned my son, whose wife later in the evening found out on the Internet what the winnings were. She was given a number for me to phone and find out what to do next. I hardly slept at all that night. I was dividing the sum mentally between members of the family and treating relatives and friends, while still finding it difficult to believe that I had actually won a jackpot prize.

On Sunday morning I phoned the given number. I was asked the number of my ticket, and an appointment was made for me to go to the lottery headquarters on the following Tuesday at 2 p.m. The person on the phone explained to me exactly how to get there.

I took a train to London on that day with my daughter wearing the ticket inside a little pouch hanging round her neck on a string, under her clothes. Losing it at that stage would have been a real disaster. We arrived at Trafalgar Square, stood in front of Nelson's Column, facing the same way as Nelson's feet (as instructed on the phone) then moved towards a large corner building with the name 'Camelot' above it.

At the entrance we were taken to a desk, where we had to show identification papers; and next we were ushered into a sitting room, where an assistant met us and asked us to follow her. After what seemed an endless walk through corridors, we went down some stairs. It reminded me of my visit to the Tower of London many years earlier, and the word *dungeons* passed through my mind. At last we entered a room which hardly reflected the fortunes that this organisation deals with every day.

The room was rather dark, the furniture old-fashioned and not matching, and the general appearance was rather depressing. There was a tap attached to the wall. They probably had people fainting when they heard the amount of their winnings. We were left in that room for what seemed a very long time. Eventually a lady appeared, introduced herself as Allison and filled in a form with more details than one needs when applying for a passport. She disappeared again, probably to check my identity details. If I had not already known what my winnings were, I would have needed a glass of water by then.

Allison came back for another talk and finished with "Are you all right?"

Fearing the worst, she prepared herself to run to the water tap to revive me.

I sympathise with people who go there not knowing what they have won. I did not disclose that I knew, still fearing that there might be a mistake somewhere and I might come out with nothing. Eventually the assistant came out with the sum that I knew and asked me if I minded her taking a photograph of me. She reassured me that it was only for their records, in case they needed to prove that they had given the money to the right person.

Cups of tea and biscuits were offered, and Allison went out to bring the cheque.

During our next session with her she gave us a lot of advice. She said we should walk out of the building and make our way without talking to anyone; I should go to my bank first thing in the morning, talk to the manager and deposit the cheque. She promised not to use my case for advertising, wished me good luck and walked us up the stairs from the 'dungeon' and through the long corridors to the exit.

We walked fast towards the station with the cheque safely hanging round my daughter's neck. We were told that twenty-two people had the same winning numbers on their tickets. Were their tickets delivered as junk mail, or did they choose the winning numbers themselves? I shall never know.

The moral of this story: never underestimate junk mail.

DO CHILDREN'S STORIES HAVE A MORAL EFFECT ON CHILDREN?

In 1967 I started a three-year primary course at the college of education in Southsea. That was the year when the Plowden Report on education was first published. There had been many reports and acts on the subject of education in the past. These, since 1905, had increased the power of teachers to choose and work out their own teaching methods.

The 1944 Act confirmed what great educators like Rousseau, Pestalozzi and others were trying to communicate for years – that there was a need to educate children according to 'their age, ability and aptitude'.

Most of the changes that took place in the following twenty years applied mainly to secondary schools. In 1964 the Schools' Council met to evaluate the changes. One of its subcommittees had done extensive research on how children learn. As a result it became apparent to them that no amount of effort spent on the improvement of secondary education could be beneficial until primary school education provided a sound basis for it. Lady Plowden published the committee's findings in the Plowden Report. Primary-school teachers were advised to read it.

For my final essay at the college of education in 1969 I chose to make a comparison between Plato's *Republic* and the Plowden Report. The similarities between them were quite surprising. Both reports stressed the importance of primary education.

Plato was born in Athens around 427 BC, two years after the

death of Pericles, which marked the end of the Golden Age for Athens and the beginning of twenty-six years of political decline, defeat in wars and revolution and six years of plague. As a young man Plato had been a pupil and a friend of Socrates for nine years. Socrates, with his unique way of teaching, tried to make people think more deeply. His method was based on asking questions in the hope that he would change people's attitude and their way of thinking. His teaching was misunderstood as being subversive and he was sentenced to death by poisoning by the government of the time. The death of Socrates was the turning point in Plato's life.

Plato, an admirer of Socrates, was also convinced that, to restore order, a new moral code was necessary. He wanted to create a society in which that moral code would prevail. He felt that it was impossible to change the attitude of the present politicians, but he believed that he could reform people's way of life by changing their way of thinking. He wrote the *Republic,* in which he elaborated on all aspects of children's upbringing.

Plato's concern was to train children right from the beginning in discipline and good manners in order that they would become good rulers. He wanted this training to be offered to all children. He wanted to put children, according to their abilities, into three categories: 'Bronze', 'Silver' and 'Gold' with the chance of moving up to a higher category. The final result would be that the children would become the 'Ordinary Citizens', the 'Guardians' and the 'Rulers' respectively.

One important part of the *Republic* covered Plato's ideas about children's stories. He believed that Homer's stories about the gods were corrupting the young. He thought that God could be good only, and he was disturbed by the way that gods were presented in anything but a godlike way. In Plato's opinion, poets as well as artists should represent virtuous character in their work. If they would not comply, they should be forbidden to practise their art.

Plato wrote that children cannot distinguish between what is allegory and what is not; that first impressions leave a permanent mark; that it is of the utmost importance that the first stories they hear should aim at producing the right moral effect. Plato called art good or bad according to what it portrayed, and not according to how it portrayed it.

The Plowden Report also considered that children's stories should supply children with a moral basis. On the other hand they doubted that it was necessary or desirable to connect this aspect of education to theology. They argued, however, that if religious belief was to serve moral education, other than as a weapon of terror, it ought to provide models for the children to imitate as well as providing the idea of a superior Guide whom they could freely choose to follow.

The Plowden Report was not adamant like Plato in its recommendations, because it recognised that children in real life come across ugly and frightening as well as pleasant events. The effects of real situations cannot be obliterated by forbidding the reading and hearing of the 'wrong' stories. They conclude that stories that are told to children, or read by them, are valuable. They develop the child's imagination and feeling of sympathy. They also enable the child to enter another personality and situation, which is a characteristic of childhood and a fundamental condition for good social relationships. Through literature, children feel forward to the experiences, the hopes and fears that await them in adult life. Both Plato and Plowden arrived at the conclusion that no story could have as strong an effect upon children's conduct as the examples which they personally encounter.

Today the questions still remain: Are children's stories part of the various means consciously used by adults in the process of educating children? What is the aim of writers of children's stories? If the aim of education is character building, could that be also the aim of children's stories?

OBLIVION

I must have been in my front garden for a little longer than I intended. One afternoon, a few years ago, I went out to close the garden gate, which had been left open by the refuse collectors. I could enter my front garden only by this gate, which was next to the front door of my house. I had left the front door open because I intended to come straight back into the house.

My next-door neighbour saw me through her bedroom window and knocked on the glass to attract my attention. She indicated to me to wait. She came out into her front garden and we – standing on either side of the fence – engaged in one of those chats that pay no attention to the passing of time.

Soon my concentration in our conversation became distracted by a smell of burning.

"I can't understand why some people have to light fires in such small back gardens. They can't have that much garden refuse to dispose of," I said to the neighbour.

"I can't smell anything," was her answer, and she carried on from where I had interrupted her while the burning smell was getting stronger by the second.

I became anxious, fearing that there was a real fire in one of the gardens nearby.

"There must be a barbecue on fire somewhere near here," I insisted.

The smell reminded me of food, but I could get no positive

response from my neighbour, who was anxious to finish what she was talking about.

Minutes passed and to add to my anxiety the sound of a fire engine, faint at first and becoming louder as it was approaching, suggested that the fire was nearby. As the sound started getting faint again I felt relieved that at least my immediate neighbours were not affected.

A few minutes later I again heard a fire engine coming our way.

I thought, 'The fire engine is either going round in circles or a second fire engine is coming to its assistance."

"Can you smell anything now?" I asked my good neighbour, taking advantage of a short silence while she was waiting for an answer to a question that had escaped my attention.

"Yes," she said, "I can. Someone's frying pan is on fire."

Suddenly I had a horrible thought. Her words had caused the penny to drop.

I just said to the neighbour, "The bacon – under the grill!" and I ran in a great hurry out of the garden, through the front door of the house, along the long corridor and into the kitchen.

A small amount of smoke was coming out of the grill pan.

At that moment there was a loud knock on the back door. Still holding the grill pan I opened the door and came face-to-face with two of the tallest firemen I had ever seen.

One of them asked, "Is there a fire here?"

I put my most innocent face on and I answered, pointing to the cinders in the grill pan, "No, this is it – just some burnt bacon. Who called you?" I asked.

"A young student who lives opposite. From his window he saw flames coming out of your cooker," answered the polite and patient fireman.

My instinct of self-defence had another go at searching for an excuse, and I came out with "I was in the front garden for only a few minutes."

I have appreciated his last remark ever since: "You are lucky to have such good neighbours."

My house was situated on a corner where three roads met, and each of the roads had a No. 47. One of these roads was my address while my house entrance, on which my '47' was displayed, was round the corner in one of the other roads. Is there any wonder the fire-engine driver had trouble finding the house?

As I was closing the back door a passer-by had the last word: "There is a £14 fine for false calls!"

The confusing address.

PLATO'S TRUTH

My kitchen window faces east. On the window sill, in the middle, there are three small flowerpots with pretty miniature roses in bloom. A succulent plant stands on the left-hand end of the window sill and a cactus on the right. The cactus is a very old one that I have been nursing for years. In spite of my efforts to make it comfortable it has never looked happy. Lately I noticed that its long, unruly leaves – or are they branches? – with their prickly edges were turning red.

I asked myself, 'Do cacti change colour when they start giving up living? Shall I be able to save it, or will it die?'

I recalled the various window sills it had occupied during its uneventful existence. It had always lived in the corner supported by the windowpane and the wall, almost hidden by the drawn curtain; a string tied round the 'branches' has acted as an added support.

Then one morning, at around eleven o'clock, the light-cream, cotton kitchen curtains, which are rather loosely woven and unlined, showed a beautiful spectacle. My first reaction was "I must draw this!" but I soon realised that the picture would change faster than I could get my sketchbook and pencil ready, so I decided to take one or two photographs and write about it instead.

The wooden bars between the windowpanes behind cast their shadows on the curtains, making an undulating pattern on them, and against this pattern I could see the silhouettes of my pot plants. Overnight, almost every 'branch' end of the cactus had produced a beautiful, large, red flower, and I saw the cactus in bloom for the first time as a glorious shadow. This blossoming probably explains the turning red of the branches beforehand.

I was so glad to have had a lie-in that morning and to have entered the kitchen at the moment when a strong sun had managed to break through the clouds and to hit the kitchen window. I normally draw the curtains much earlier, but the reading of someone's interesting autobiographical book kept me in bed listening to Radio Four.

The spectacle of shadows on the kitchen curtains brings to mind the story of the cave which Plato mentioned when he was writing his report on education. In Plato's story a prisoner stands in complete darkness. In front of him there is a curtain, on which he sees the shadows of puppets. The prisoner moves into the next space, where he sees the puppets themselves in twilight. He then moves into the next space, where there is the strong light of the sun. There he sees things as they really are. The prisoner never wants to be in the darkness again.

The flowering cactus shadows.

Plato considered that the most important ingredient of living was the need of aiming at 'the good' – the true picture. His philosophy was based on the belief that the only good life was the life spent trying to see the light, as we say today. There is a line in a wartime song that has stayed in my memory ever since. It says, 'I'm beginning to see the light.' There is also another line, probably from around the same time, that illustrates the prisoner's thoughts after he saw the light. That line is 'Don't fence me in'.

Plato's story of the cave makes one think that during his time ideas about the aims of education were not very different from how they are now, 2,500 years later. Plato compares the process of learning with the gradual moving from complete darkness to the strongest light. He believes that for everything there is a perfect form, that, whatever one does, one must be aiming at the 'true image', which is at the back of one's mind, just as the painter paints his picture according to the image in his own mind.

The flowering cactus.

FALSE ALARM

It happened during an afternoon sometime in the late 1980s. On my way to the supermarket I passed a charity shop which displayed a smart, black briefcase just outside its entrance, on a small table. A well-known name on a disc near the opening of the case, and the low price of £5 on a ticket attached to it, made it irresistible to me. After all, was it not exactly what I had always wanted? Or was it?

I had never imagined myself carrying one of these briefcases in public, but I had seen men in black suits holding that prestigious item in one hand and a long black umbrella in the other – not forgetting the black hat – boarding commuter trains between London and its suburbs.

I am a rather tidy person and I thought the briefcase would be ideal for keeping all important family and personal papers together, in one place. So I picked up the smart briefcase, entered the charity shop, paid the £5 to the friendly assistant and carried on on my way to the supermarket.

I placed the briefcase on the floor next to my own trolley, near the large window of the supermarket, then I collected a supermarket trolley and proceeded to concentrate on trying to remember the items on my unwritten shopping list, while resisting the temptation of offers of 'two for one' for unwanted bargains.

Shopping done, I pushed the supermarket trolley next to my own trolley and started transferring the items. I was oblivious to the fact that an elderly lady standing near me, probably waiting for a lift home, was following my movements.

Suddenly I heard a quiet voice saying, "That is two for one, dear. You should have another one free."

It was a small item – not worth rejoining the queue to get it – so I pulled down the cover of my trolley, thanked the helpful lady, turned towards the exit and made my way home.

It must have taken me about fifteen minutes, probably a little longer, to walk home, put the shopping away and sit down to a cup of tea. Then I suddenly realised that I had left the briefcase behind. In a great hurry I put on my coat and shoes and rushed out of the front door, walking as fast as I could, hoping that nobody had fancied it, as I had earlier on. It was there to be picked up by the wrong person – this time for free.

My house was only five minutes' walk from the corner of the street, and the supermarket was three small shops further down the road on the left. As I approached the corner I noticed that people had gathered on the pavement. I soon recognised the supermarket assistants. I thought that one of those safety exercises was in progress.

I felt a little irritated at the thought of having to wait for some time before I could retrieve my briefcase or even before I could find out whether it was still there.

I was just ready to ask the supermarket assistants what was going on when I heard one of them saying, "Here she is!" while pointing her finger at me. Just out of the blue a policeman appeared, and said quietly and politely, "Will you please come with me?"

For a second a picture of handcuffs flashed through my mind.

During the next few seconds I seemed to be in one of those dreams in which senseless things happen at the speed of light. The policeman was marching me towards the side entrance of the supermarket. There were police cars parked at both ends of the road, which was cordoned off while policemen were redirecting the traffic. One policeman was talking on his radio. An ambulance was waiting at the other side of a tape which was stretched across the width of the road.

With the uniformed escort by my side I walked, in a daze, through the groups of evacuated staff and customers of the three little shops that preceded the supermarket: a wool shop, a shoe shop and a Chinese restaurant. I avoided looking at the assistants, whose shops I had visited at times during the previous twenty-five years.

I wondered why we passed the main entrance of the supermarket and carried on to the side entrance, although by then I had realised that it was not a matter of a safety exercise, that it was a false alarm and that, to my horror, I had caused it.

Now it was the turn of my defence instinct to get into action. I thought, 'In this full-of-electronic-miracles age should they not have a means of finding out from a distance whether there was anything suspicious in that case?'

I heard later that men from the Bomb Squad were present, which explains why the police cars parked on both sides of the road were not exactly the same – an observation I made when I first arrived at the scene. I felt so thankful that I had not left it until the next day to claim back the briefcase. Luckily, I lived only minutes away from the supermarket.

From the side entrance of the supermarket we entered what looked like a storeroom and the policeman brought me back to earth by asking, "Did you leave anything behind when you came shopping earlier on?"

"Yes," I answered. "I left a black briefcase that I had just bought at the charity shop on my way here."

"Is anything inside it?" he asked.

"As far as I know it is empty. I have not opened it yet," I said.

"Are you sure?"

'How can I be sure,' I thought, 'if I have not opened it yet?'

We made our way to the inside of the main entrance of the shop and there it was! We stopped in front of the case, which was standing innocently just where I had deposited it.

"Is it yours?"

I could not stop apologising; the policeman was very sympathetic. With shaking hands I opened the case to reveal the lack of content. After more apologies, I could not walk away fast enough.

Dreading to parade again through the patiently waiting onlookers, this time carrying the briefcase, I turned left and walked the long way (probably a mile) to go home.

My main thoughts were then 'Will it be in the local newspaper tomorrow? What would be the headline? Do they know my name?'

I stayed indoors the next day, much as I wanted to buy the paper. The day after, I made my way to another supermarket at the other end of the road. As I was passing the charity shop, which was between the two supermarkets, I was hoping that the assistant was looking the other way, but I heard her saying triumphantly, "This is the lady!"

She must have been repeating the story to all her customers for the past forty-eight hours.

I decided to go inside and supply her with additional information on what had happened after she sold me the briefcase.

The first thing she said to me was "What is your name?"

"Why?" I asked.

She carried on: "Do you mind if we publish the story in our monthly magazine?"

Well, my name was exactly the detail she was not going to have!

The briefcase.